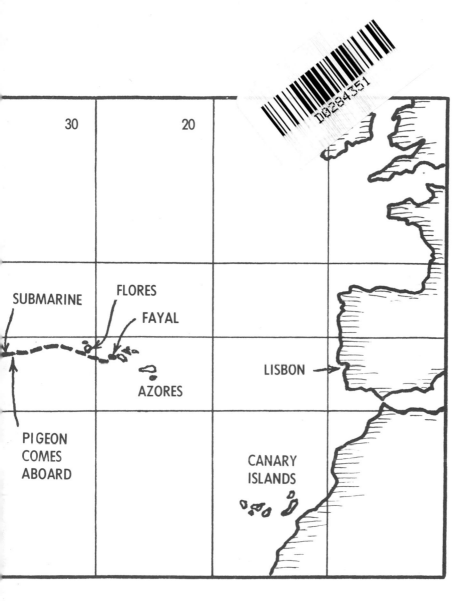

30

20

SUBMARINE

FLORES

FAYAL

LISBON →

AZORES

PIGEON
COMES
ABOARD

CANARY
ISLANDS

EAST TO
THE AZORES

EAST TO THE AZORES

A Guide to Offshore Passage-Making

BY RICHARD HENDERSON

With Illustrations by the Author

INTERNATIONAL MARINE PUBLISHING COMPANY

OTHER BOOKS BY RICHARD HENDERSON

First Sail For Skipper
Hand, Reef and Steer
Dangerous Voyages of Captain William Andrews (Ed.)
Sail and Power (with B. S. Dunbar)
The Racing-Cruiser
Sea Sense
The Cruiser's Compendium
Singlehanded Sailing
Better Sailing

All photographs by Rip or Sally Henderson except where otherwise indicated.

Copyright © 1978
by International Marine Publishing Company
Library of Congress Catalog Card Number 77-91878
International Standard Book Number 0-87742-097-1
Typeset by A & B Typesetters, Inc., Concord, New Hampshire
Printed and bound by The Maple Press Company, York, Pennsylvania

Published by International Marine Publishing Company
21 Elm Street, Camden, Maine 04843

To Sally, Sarah, and Rip —

the best possible crew

Contents

PREFACE

This book tells of a cruise in the Ohlson 38 sloop *Kelpie* from Gibson Island, Maryland, to Fayal, in the Azores, in the late spring and early summer of 1975. The crew was a family—my wife and myself (I suppose we are middle-aged) and our son and daughter (they supposed they were adults).

We made our careful preparations, embarked, had our gales and calms, our fair share of beautiful moonlit nights and glorious sailing days, had the thrill of making landfall after nearly a month at sea and the satisfaction of successfully completing the passage we had planned without serious mishap.

Among the annals of small boat voyaging, our cruise is commonplace indeed.

It was, of course, an important and exciting adventure to us. Yet that is perhaps insufficient reason to write a book about the cruise.

This book is a little different from the usual cruise story. It is not a chronological log but a topical treatment with each chapter focusing on one aspect of the planning and execution of the passage. Another difference is that the book goes into some of the nitty-gritty details of gear, supplies, preparations, and boat handling. The brand names of equipment are mentioned, and I have no reservations about saying what we liked or didn't like. My attempt has been to make the book useful to others who are planning a similar venture.

While fitting out, we read or reread dozens of cruising accounts in search of practical information, but we were often frustrated by lack of details. What we considered essential gear, the life raft for example, was often not named, described, or discussed, and techniques such as self-steering, changing sails, and raising sprouts were seldom dealt with in any depth. This book attempts to supply the kind of information we were seeking when making preparations.

Not that the narrative part has been omitted, for the whole story is told, even if in a non-chronological way, and I've tried to convey our emotional reactions to the vicissitudes. We all kept personal diaries, and there are occasional quotes from them to express the thoughts and feelings of each member of our family crew. In short, the attempt has been made to combine a narrative with practical matters, to present an in-depth case study of family ocean cruising. It is my hope that some who read these pages will be encouraged to plan and carry out their own cruises.

Richard Henderson
Gibson Island, Maryland

1

A PLAN

or

Quirks of Fate

The crushing wind and battering spray on my back seemed to pin me against the wheel. Huge breaking seas came charging up from astern, like attacking monsters with bared white fangs. Every so often one would crash aboard and half fill the cockpit. There was an appalling din of tumbling water, flapping cloth, and the metallic tattoo of halyards beating the aluminum mast. Above the high-pitched moan of the spars each wire in the rigging was screaming its own dissonant tune. It was June 21st (my son's birthday), and we were running under bare pole before what appeared to be a Force 10 gale near the mid-Atlantic.

The storm seemed interminable. It was gradually wearing us down, leaving us exhausted. To add to our anxieties, the boat had a mysterious persistent leak that required regular pumping. I had been at the helm for several hours, fighting the wheel, trying to avoid the breaking crests while keeping the stern up to the wind. My family were battened down below, but after one frightful smash from a sea, I noticed the companionway hatch being jerkily slid back. My wife, Sally, slowly and carefully emerged, fully garbed in her foul weather gear and safety harness.

"What are you doing on deck?" I screamed. She did not say a word but crawled over to me, hanging on for dear life, and snapped her safety line next to mine around the compass pedestal. Then in the most calm and almost casual voice she said, "I have decided to die with you." There was no sign of hysterics or panic, but she was absolutely convinced that we could not survive. That moment had to be the low point of our cruise. It was then that I asked myself the question which sooner or later, many a blue water sailor asks: "What the hell are we doing here?"

For a brief moment, I felt wretchedly guilty for having brought my family along and for subjecting them to such anxieties and physical stress. Yet Sally and both children had wanted to make the trip, and when the gale was over, we all agreed that it had been one of the greatest experiences of our lives, one we had shared in a most intimate way, and one none of us would ever forget. Moreover, we had gained a new kind of respect for each other and a much greater confidence in ourselves. At the risk of sounding overly dramatic, I'll say that we even developed a somewhat different, more intense appreciation of life.

Our passage, like many others, started with a dream. For me the dream had come early in life when, as a teenager, I had been fascinated by the writings of Slocum, Voss, Robinson, and other famous small-boat voyagers. Although I had no particular aspirations to emulate those great sailors (my adventure quotient is much too low), I did begin to envision a blue water cruise in my future. As the years passed, I did a fair amount of inland and coastal cruising as well as a bit of offshore sailing, but those activities did nothing to diminish the urge to make a significant ocean passage in my own boat.

There were other motivations, of course, aside from the desire to fulfill an early dream. The principal one came after I was married and had children. It occurred to me that a long ocean cruise would be a splendid family experience, one that would draw us very close together and diminish the generation gap. There would be ample time for lengthy conversations and a rare opportunity for Sally and me to really get to know our children. Then too, there was the fun of planning the trip together, and the attraction of looking forward to sharing a real adventure, which is all too rare in our modern, sheltered civilization.

As for Sally, she has always had a moderately high adventure quotient or Ulysses factor, call it what you will, and she is a compulsive traveler, ready to go anywhere at the drop of a hat. She was forever pestering me to go abroad with her, and I would always reply half seriously that the best way to get there would be in our own boat. The thought eventually began to sink into her mind, and after our children had sufficiently grown to be able hands on a boat, Sally was ready to call my bluff.

Our son, Rip, was a naturally good sailor, and he was most enthusiastic over the prospect of going to sea. His younger sister, Sarah, was not so sure. As a youngster she had always been more interested in tennis than sailing, and I had never tried to force her into boats. Nevertheless, she thought our seagoing plan would be an exciting experience, and she could not bear the thought of being left behind.

In the late summer of 1973, Sally and I came to the realization that if we didn't make our ocean cruise soon, we probably never would. We were approaching 50 years of age, and our children were becoming more independent and beginning to make plans of their own. There were probably not many more years when we would all be together as a family and when we all could spare the time simultaneously to make such a trip.

One Sunday morning, over a leisurely breakfast, we began discussing the practical aspects of our project. Where would we go? How much would such a trip cost? What kind of a boat should we have? How much time could we spare? What kind of preparations would be necessary?

After much discussion, we decided that one summer was all

the time we could afford, and we wanted to go as far as we could, yet still allow time for travel on shore and sightseeing in a foreign country. Our home base was Gibson Island on the Chesapeake Bay, near Annapolis, Maryland, and from that starting point the choice of destinations seemed to be either Bermuda, the West Indies, the Azores, or Europe. Bermuda was out, because Sally and I had already made that passage on a sailboat, and the distance was too short. We had also spent time in the West Indies, and a passage there would not really take us out into the middle of the Atlantic. Another consideration at the time was that we were not at all skilled in celestial navigation, and a landfall in the northern West Indies islands with their outlying shoals and reefs seemed more difficult than the mountainous islands of the Azores. We really wanted to make a transatlantic crossing, and visit Europe without leaving the boat abroad, but there was the problem of time. How could we sail over, travel in Europe, and bring the boat home again in the same summer? We could ship her home, but that would be expensive, troublesome, and perhaps risky in regard to boat damage and loss of gear through pilferage.

The perfect solution, we decided, would be to have a seaman friend sail the boat home, picking her up from us soon after we reached our destination, but such a person would not be easy to find. Eventually, we found him in the person of Edward Karkow, who proved to be eminently qualified. Ed was a regular member of my racing crew; he had made a transatlantic crossing previously in his own boat; he knew celestial navigation; he had run a boatyard for a while; and he was anxious to make the trip (without pay). Furthermore, he was very reliable, and I had confidence he would take good care of our boat.

We did not know whether or not we could make it all the way across to Europe. Our passage might very well have to end at the Azores, because we could not depart from Gibson Island until after the first week in June, and the boat would have to return before the beginning of the peak of the hurricane season, about the first of August. Our eventual plan was to try for Lisbon, Portugal, if the weather allowed a fast passage, but to terminate in the Azores if the trip was slow. We would call Ed Karkow from the Azores to let him know where to meet us.

During that Sunday morning breakfast, Sally and I discussed the kind of boat we should have for the trip. We already owned a stock 30-footer, a Cal 2-30. In many respects, she was very satisfactory, and we knew of a sister vessel that had made a singlehanded transatlantic crossing, but we felt she was not quite the right boat for our plans. She was a little too small and too lively in her motion. Furthermore, she was not really intended for extensive offshore work, and I preferred a slightly more robust construction with certain safety features, such as a smaller self-draining cockpit with a higher companionway sill, wider sidedecks, a mast stepped through the deck, and a diesel engine.

Sally asked me what boat I would prefer above all others, regardless of price, and it didn't take me long to think of the Ohlson 38. This boat is an unusual combination of beauty, speed, comfort, strength, and seaworthiness. Of course, every design is a compromise, and there is no such thing as a perfect boat, but the O-38 came (and still comes) very close to being ideal for our purposes. Much more will be said about the boat in Chapter 2.

That very evening after our breakfast discussion, we went to a cocktail party where I saw a yacht broker friend. I couldn't resist asking him what used Ohlson 38s were selling for, but he replied that he'd never heard of the boat. I knew that used O-38s seldom came on the U.S. market, and thinking that we could not afford one anyway, I decided then and there to push that particular boat out of my mind. Two weeks later, however, my yacht broker friend called to say that he knew of an O-38 for sale in Maine.

It often happens that certain events, even major turning points in one's life, are determined by quirks of fate that seem insignificant at the time. So it was with us when Sally and I drove our automobile north in the early fall of 1973. We were on our way to Mystic, Connecticut, to do some research at the Mystic Seaport Museum. Our conversation was an absorbing one about

Designed by E. Ohlson

Length O.A.	36'8"	11.43 m
Length W.L.	26'6"	8.00 m
Beam	10'3"	3.12 m
Draft	5'7"	1.70 m
Ballast	2 ton 13½ cwt 2800 Kg	

The Ohlson 38 hull and rig similar to ours (for headsails carried on the cruise, see Figure 10-1).

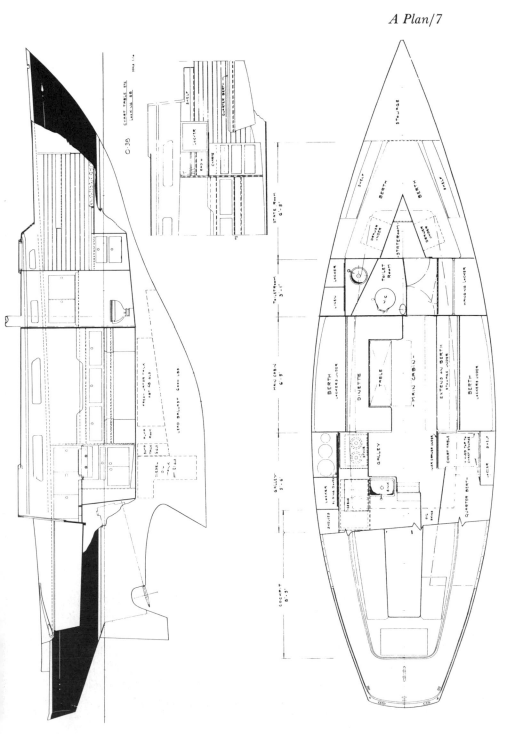

Ohlson 38 hull profile and arrangement plans. Note: The head on our boat is raised above the waterline to guard against flooding in the event of a broken check valve.

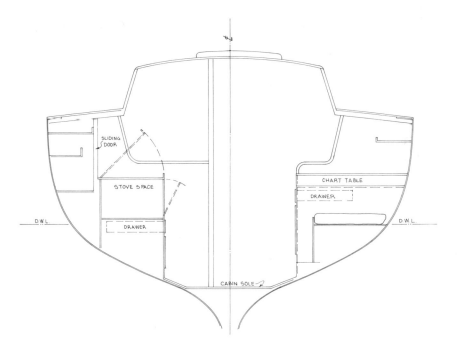

The seakindly but moderately powerful section of the Ohlson 38 at station 3 (slightly more than 5 feet abaft the midship section). Note the easy curves at the garboards that give strength to the after end of the keel. (Courtesy of the designer, Einar Ohlson.)

the ideal boat for our future, when suddenly we found ourselves at the road sign that pointed the way to Mystic. On a sudden impulse, Sally suggested that we continue straight ahead and drive to Maine for a look at the Ohlson 38. Had it been raining or the traffic bad, I would have resisted, but it was a beautiful day with the foliage beginning to show its autumn colors, so I enthusiastically agreed to her suggestion, and we headed the car for points "downeast."

The Ohlson 38, named *Mandalay,* was at Hinckley's yard in Southwest Harbor, Maine, and she was shown to us by a tall, bearded sailor/naval architect, John Letcher, who was later to become a good friend. Sally and I fell in love with the boat at first sight. She had been a charter boat in recent years and had not received an abundance of "tender loving care," but what deficiencies she had were purely cosmetic. Basically, she appeared to be sound, and I was actually pleased that there was a need for some cleaning and superficial repairs, because that

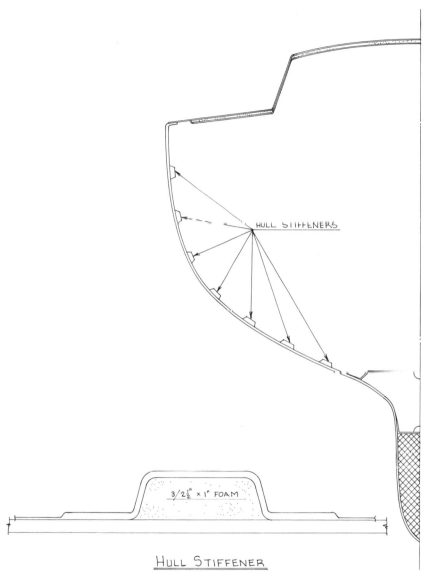

3/2½" × 1" FOAM

HULL STIFFENER

Midship section of the Ohlson 38 that shows her 14 (7 per side) hull stiffeners. These are full-length longitudinal stringers constructed of fiberglass filled with polyurethane foam. The integral fiberglass keel tanks also add support in the garboard region.

might indicate the boat could be had for somewhat less than the asking price. It turned out that the owner was abroad and was most anxious to sell.

Kelpie sailing on the Chesapeake Bay during the summer of 1974. Note the high boom that is well above the head of anyone standing in the cockpit or even on a cockpit seat. (Fred Grell)

The second minor quirk of fate, aside from our spontaneous decision to bypass Mystic, came when we arrived at the Hinckley yard. A telephone call came for me from Annapolis, Maryland. The call was from a yacht broker saying that he had a good offer on our Cal 2-30, which we had recently put up for sale. We could not imagine how the broker knew we were in Maine, because Sally and I had told no one we were going there. Our downeast trip was a real spur-of-the-moment decision. Later we learned the broker had simply played a hunch that we might be looking at the Ohlson 38. At any rate, all the pieces fell into place while we were at Hinckley's. We found the boat we wanted, we received a realistic offer on our present boat, and we made an offer on the O-38 subject to survey and the sale of our Cal 2-30. To make a long story short, the owner of *Mandalay* accepted our offer, the boat passed her survey, our Cal was sold, and we became the proud owners of a handsome Ohlson 38.

Near the end of October, *Mandalay* was brought down the coast by Sandro Vitelli, a yacht deliverer, who was working for Hinckley. We wanted to sail our new boat home ourselves but could not do so on account of prior commitments. *Mandalay* was supposed to be delivered to Gibson Island, but Sandro ran into some very heavy weather offshore and had to end his delivery at Cape May, New Jersey. Despite his hard trip down the coast with gale-force winds, Sandro was very enthusiastic about *Mandalay*. He said she was fast, tough, and a good sea boat, which was most encouraging to hear. Early in November, during a bitterly cold northwesterly spell, Sally and I, together with Ed Karkow, were able to pick the boat up at Cape May and bring her home. We arrived at Gibson Island after dark, in a rain squall, and without an engine, which had "packed up" earlier. It was a thrill tacking the new boat into our harbor at night and picking up the mooring under sail. It almost seemed like the boat knew she was going to her new home.

Now that we had what we considered was the proper craft, the next part of our plan was long-range preparations for the ocean passage. We would spend the following summer getting to know the boat, modifying her for the trip, accumulating equipment, learning navigation, and so forth. Then, hopefully, we would set off on the cruise in the early summer of 1975. Our individual responsibilities were roughly assigned as follows: I would be the skipper, carpenter, handy man, and primary navigator; Sally would be the back-up navigator, primary cook, provisioner, and back-up medic; Rip would be the foredeck man, medic, back-up cook, and photographer; and Sarah was to be in charge of entertainment, travel research, sanitation, exotic cooking, and stowage. As it turned out, Sarah went away to college and so did not have much time to devote to some of her cruise assignments; but Sally, Rip, and I were able to fill in for her where necessary. Once the basic plan was decided on, we could look forward to preparing the boat and ourselves. Almost half the fun of a voyage comes from the learning of new skills, studies relating to the enterprise, organization, and careful preparations.

2

THE BOAT
or
Easy Pleasure

There is little doubt that many of today's mass-produced cruising sailboats are not at all ideal for extended work offshore. They may be fine for short cruises on sheltered waters, but for lengthy exposure to heavy weather in the open sea . . . forget it; the risk is too great. On the other hand, I have never felt that one needs a heavy Colin Archer double-ender or a high freeboard motorsailer to make a passage offshore. A stock racing-cruiser can be a fine sea boat without sacrifice to sailing performance, *provided* she is a wholesome, moderate type, well designed and strongly built.

What we were looking for when we bought our Ohlson 38 was a versatile boat, one we could safely take anywhere offshore, yet one that was fast enough for occasional racing. We wanted a handsome boat that was a smart sailer, especially to windward, and one that would be easy to handle and maintain. That's a lot

The sleek underbody of an Ohlson 38 showing the swept forefoot and integral keel. The lateral plane is a compromise between low wetted area for speed and keel length for directional stability. This configuration also gives a low center of gravity while allowing ample leeway when lying ahull to minimize the risk of tripping. (Courtesy Buzz White.)

to ask from any boat nowadays, but I felt that the O-38 could meet those basic requirements, and she has more than lived up to our expectations.

Features I consider essential or at least highly desirable for an offshore boat are as follows:

Strength: This is probably the foremost requirement because the boat must be able to withstand heavy weather and stay in one piece. Construction need not be tremendously heavy, but the hull must be solidly put together, rigid enough to resist flexing and panting (oil canning), and sufficiently thick to survive collisions with flotsam or sea life.

Stability: There should be sufficient keel ballast and a low enough center of gravity of the hull to assure a high range of stability and recovery from a severe knockdown or capsize. Typical deep keel racing-cruisers usually meet this requirement, but some high freeboard cruisers and motorsailer types with shallow keels, low ballast-displacement ratios, and lofty deck houses and cockpits are too vulnerable to being rolled over at sea. For me, an important requirement is the ability to lie ahull (broadside to the wind and seas under bare poles) in heavy weather, but without a decent range of stability, the risk of capsizing is too great.

Watertightness: For obvious reasons it is essential that a sinkable boat remain watertight under any conditions she could possibly encounter. This means that there should be no vulnerable deep fin or skeg that could crack or be broken off and allow the flooding of the hull. I prefer a swept-back forefoot and keel to alleviate impact in the event the boat should happen to strike a submerged floating object head-on. There should be a small self-bailing cockpit well with large drains and the house should have small "unbreakable" windows. Of course, all openings into the hull must be capable of being closed completely and easily.

Seakindliness: This is a complex and somewhat controversial subject that cannot be discussed in a few words, but I feel strongly that extremes of hull shape and displacement should be shunned. Moderate displacement avoids the sluggishness and lack of buoyancy of extremely heavy boats while avoiding the quick motion and lack of momentum of extremely light boats. A hull shape of moderate proportions would have such characteristics as: medium overhangs for reserve buoyancy without slamming; a soft (rounded) bilge for strength, resistance to pounding, and (in combination with moderate, slow-curving body depth amidships) to improve directional stability; medium beam amidships with moderate fullness carried into the ends for good tracking, the damping of pitching, and resistance to pitch-poling; and a keel of moderate length, short enough for good helm response and low wetted area, but long enough to track well.

Rig suitability: The rig most suitable for shorthanded offshore work should emphasize reliability and avoid extremes in height and sail area. The masts must be sturdy and well stayed, while the sails should be sufficiently large and aerodynamically efficient for effective drive under all conditions but not so lofty or large in area as to cause tenderness or make handling difficult. An inboard rig is best from the standpoint of safety in sail handling.

By and large, the Ohlson 38 meets all of the above requirements, which is remarkable when you consider the way she performs against some of the new IOR (International Offshore Rule) racing machines that I, for one, would never think about boarding for a distant shorthanded ocean cruise.

Designed by the famous Swedish naval architect Einar Ohlson, the O-38 is a fiberglass boat molded by the Tyler Boat Company in England and finished elsewhere, normally either by Alexander Robertson and Sons in Scotland or by the Ohlson Brothers in Sweden. Our boat was completed by the Swedish yard, and not surprisingly, the joiner work is superb. I have always admired the design work of Einar Ohlson, because most of his boats with which I'm familiar are versatile, aesthetically pleasing, and unusually well balanced. Perhaps the sensitivity to balance comes from the fact that Ohlson was one of the best designers of meter boats, and those craft are noted for a fine balance that changes relatively little with heel.

There are several things I like about the O-38's construction. First, it is built to rules and standards set forth by Lloyd's Register of Shipping. Of course, it is perfectly possible to have a sound boat that is not built to Lloyd's, but when high standards are followed there is greater assurance that there are no hidden flaws. Second, the hull is produced by one of the most highly respected molders, the company that builds such impressive craft as the Ocean-71, which for many years was the world's largest stock fiberglass yacht. I had the pleasure of visiting the Tyler Company at Tonbridge, Kent, in 1975 and was most impressed with the operation. Hulls are carefully laid up by hand with chopped strand mat and woven rovings using clear, unadulterated resin below the waterline, which better assures correct resin saturation and limits the entrapment of air pockets or bubbles in the laminate. One can plainly see through the hull to spot any defect, and each layer is color coded to aid the layup.

Another reason I like the O-38's construction is that the hull is strengthened by extensive use of foam-filled fiberglass longitudinal stringers, which gives rigidity without excessive weight. The late naval architect and noted design critic Robert Henry once wrote: "The system of longitudinal stiffeners inside the fiberglass hull provides extra longitudinal strength, increases local stiffness, and assures that the hull will maintain its fairness. It has the disadvantage that bulkheads and interior joiner work are more difficult to fit. Most molded auxiliaries do not include this type of hull reinforcement which could lead one to believe that it is not altogether necessary. I have often wondered how many fiberglass boats would fit into their original molds after they have been sailed hard for four or five years. It would be a safe bet that many lightly constructed classes have changed shape enough so that they would be a far cry from a neat fit. This is a point that probably never will be proven, but if I had my choice I'd take the hull with well engineered reinforcements, as in the Ohlson-38."

In the construction of the O-38's cabin trunk and deck, there are a number of choices. The most handsome is a mahogany trunk with teak deck, but our boat is all fiberglass, which I prefer because of low maintenance, minimum leakage, and lighter weight above the topsides to provide greater stability. Actually, the boat is so good-looking and the trunk and hull so harmonious that there is no need for a lot of wood, other than a minimum of teak trim. The deck-trunk molding has an interior fiberglass liner, which adds to the difficulty of attaching any extra through-bolted fittings, but there is polyurethane foam between the laminate and liner to provide good insulation and prevent condensation. The cabin interior is very attractive with a lightweight mahogany ceiling. Ordinarily, I don't like a ceiling because of the difficulty in reaching the hull shell (for inspections, to reach wiring or piping, etc.), but O-38's can be unscrewed quite easily, and there are slight cracks between the ceiling planks for ventilation and to facilitate quick removal in an emergency.

The cabin arrangement for this size boat is hard to beat. There is a splendid navigator's niche with adequate chart table near the companionway and on the opposite side of the boat a U-shaped galley into which the cook can be well secured with safety belts. The galley has plenty of counter space and lockers, a gimballed three-burner stove with oven, large ice box that can easily hold a hundred pounds of ice, and a good sink near the boat's centerline which never floods during a knockdown.

There are seven bunks, two forward in a private stateroom, a quarter berth aft, and two transom berths and two pilot berths amidships in the main cabin. One of the pilot berths is a sliding type, and we only use it as a stowage area. One of the transoms slides also, which is a good feature, because it converts from a comfortable seat to a berth of any desired width (narrow bunks are best in a seaway). The other transom is part of a dinette seating arrangement that surrounds a semi-permanent dropleaf table. Our particular boat has a bulkhead-mounted charcoal heating stove with a smoke pipe leading to the deck, and this makes a very cozy arrangement in cold weather.

The head compartment is a large standup room that can be extended across the width of the boat by opening two side-by-side doors. The head can be used either with the doors closed in the athwartship position, which blocks off the accommodations, or with the doors closed in the fore-and-aft position, which allows a clear passageway fore and aft.

Stowage space is almost unbelievable, with thirty-six lockers, not counting shelves. They swallow up stores to such an extent that we were finding beer, wine and other consumables for months after our boat returned from her two-and-a-half month voyage. Even so, the largest locker (under the cockpit seat) was never completely filled.

Surprisingly, after our boat was fully loaded for the trip, she did not sink below her boot-top, and her sailing performance did not suffer to any great extent. It is not always realized that in contrast to light-weight boats, medium to heavy displacement cruisers can sail almost as well when they are heavily loaded, provided the extra weight is kept low and out of the ends.

The hull shape of the O-38 is moderate and beautiful, in the traditional sense at least. It is a pre-IOR design, and unlike some of the newer racing cruisers that seem to be wrapped around IOR measurements points for optimal rating, it does not suffer from extreme beam amidships, excessive bulging tumblehome (or bumps), pinched ends, or a chopped-off stern. There is a choice of sterns, one having a reversed and another having a traditional (non-reversed) transom. Our boat has the latter, and this is the type I prefer, not only for appearance, but also because the reversed stern is added on beyond the deck molding, thereby extending the overhang a bit too far, in my opinion, and adding weight to the stern. I think the traditional transom provides a sufficient stern counter to lengthen the sailing lines, balance the bow's overhang, and afford ample reserve buoyancy.

To the eye of a traditionalist, the O-38's sheer line might be a trifle flat, but I don't like a sheer that dips too low amidships,

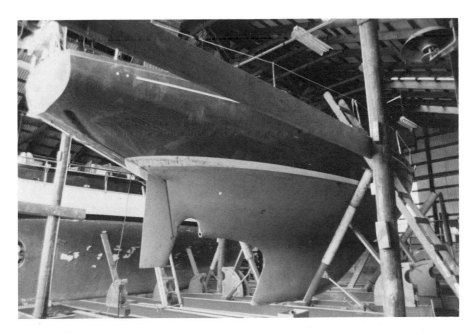

Kelpie hauled out at the Gibson Island Yacht Yard. This stern view shows the overhanging counter and small rudder attached to a shallow integral skeg that has a wide base flaring into a slight bustle. (Bob Cochran)

because it often results in the lee deck being awash when the boat is heeled.

The keel is not unlike certain fish fins that nature has perfected through evolution. It may not be as efficient for producing lift as the latest high-aspect-ratio fin keels, but there is one debatable theory that the swept forefoot or keel slope does help in preventing water flow from the high pressure lee side to the weather side of the keel. Aerodynamicist John Morwood discussed the theory in the Amateur Yacht Research Society's "The Hydrodynamics of Lateral Resistance."

Hydrodynamics aside, however, there are other plaudits for such a keel shape. There is the safety factor (already mentioned) in the swept forefoot; the length permits good helm response with little sacrifice to directional stability; there is room in the keel for tanks and a bilge water sump, and the shape allows the ballast to be placed low for very nearly the lowest center of gravity for a given weight of ballast. A most important consideration, in my opinion, is the fact that the keel shape allows considerable leeway when there is no headway (in contrast to a long keel), and this is all but essential for lying ahull in heavy weather because otherwise the boat could trip on her keel and roll over.

The rudder is surprisingly small, and it is hung on a small skeg. I don't like deep high-aspect-ratio skegs on seagoing boats because of the possibility of breakage, but the O-38's is shallow and very strong. There is a slight bustle or swelling of the area just forward of the skeg, which is not only helpful to hydrodynamic flow, but also provides a strong supporting base for the skeg-rudder assembly.

In recent years the O-38's rig has been modernized. As compared with the original 1968 plan, the new rig is considerably taller, with a shorter main boom and inboard shrouds to allow closer trimming of headsails. Our boat, built in 1969, has the original rig but with a mast fourteen inches taller than standard and a shorter main boom that sheets to a mid-cockpit traveller. We have the outboard shrouds, but they seem to detract very little from windward ability. The aluminum spars are made by

Sparlight in England, and we've had no trouble with them except for breaking the mainsail's outhaul fitting.

As for sailing performance, the O-38 excels when beating in a moderate breeze. She also runs well and is fast reaching provided she has enough heel to submerge part of her overhangs to increase waterline length. Our 27-day passage from Cape May to Fayal was not fast by any means, but we were sailing shorthanded, and the boat was sailed very conservatively with sail reduced most nights. Furthermore, we were heavily loaded and dragging a large solid prop, and had more than our share of heavy weather, head winds, and calms. Our fastest day's run was 164 miles, which is not too bad for a boat that is 26.56 feet on the waterline, but under the right conditions with a full crew and racing sails, I feel sure we could break two hundred miles per day. On a six-hour run last summer while surfing before large seas, Sally and I, sailing the boat alone, averaged 9.18 knots in tideless conditions, and I have a photo of the log needle pinned at twelve knots, where it often remained for several seconds. Our boat is weakest in drifting conditions. She needs at least two knots or so of wind to make her move.

The log needle pinned at 12 knots while Kelpie *surfs down a sea. She was running under full main and a boomed-out jib.*

Racing the boat in Delta Class, the most popular class on the Chesapeake Bay, we have been fairly successful, finishing second in seasonal high points in 1974. Our second year of racing, in 1976, was not as successful, but we finished in the money more often than not and won two overnight races and our division in the Wednesday evening series competing against a few of the newer IOR boats. Given a decent breeze and a beat to windward in moderately smooth water, the O-38 can beat many of the hot IOR boats of comparable waterline length, and she can even hold some of the one-tonners under the right conditions. That's not too bad for a small ocean-going cruiser. But competitive or not, she's a joy to sail.

So far, this report on the O-38 has been mostly laudatory, but the boat is not perfect, simply because no boat is. However, her weaknesses are few. Some people seem to have a hard time steering her in following seas. Although our boat tracks well and doesn't tend to broach, she can be over-steered, especially with her Edson wheel, which requires little effort to turn. Perhaps a slightly larger rudder would help, but neither I nor my family has had much of a problem with the helm. Furthermore, the boat tracks well enough that she can be made to self-steer easily.

The famous singlehander Clare Francis has written that her O-38 *Robertson's Golly* is a bit tender, but I must say that I have found the opposite to be true. Most often our competitors are reefed or carrying small jibs while we are not. Our boat heels fairly easily until 25 or 30 degrees and then she stops, and it takes a piping wind to bury her rail.

Miss Francis also complained of some leaks at the hull deck connection, and our boat had this same trouble under previous ownership, but the leaks were stopped fairly well by work done at the Hinckley yard in Maine. The deck was lifted slightly on one side, the joint was packed with a rubber-like sealer (Boatlife, I think), and then the deck was refastened to the hull flange with numerous stainless steel bolts. I asked Richard Sheehan, who runs a charter fleet of O-38s in the Virgin Islands, if any of his boats had this leakage problem, and his reply was negative.

Like many modern fiberglass boats, the O-38 has its ballast encased in the keel. This is not good if you intend to go

An aerial view of **Kelpie** *beating to windward during a race on the Chesapeake Bay in conditions to her liking. Note the small cockpit well and flush hatches, which are good safety features for offshore work. (Tom Leutwiler, Daedelus Photography)*

bouncing off rocks, because the glass at the bottom of the keel is vulnerable, but repair is not difficult and the hull cannot be flooded even from a rupture. For sailing in areas where the bottom is soft, such as Chesapeake Bay, I'd far rather have the encased ballast, because it avoids the problems associated with external ballast . . . keel bolt leakage and corrosion and the difficulty of keeping a smooth keel surface.

We sometimes have a minor annoyance with engine vibration, but I have found this is easy to control by changing the RPM, simply slowing down or speeding up a bit. The two-cylinder diesel, a Volvo MD2, is only rated at 15 horsepower (European system), but it drives the boat at a good five knots, and it is marvelously economical, using only about a third of a gallon of fuel per hour. I must say that we are greatly comforted by the safety of a diesel, and it has proven to be reliable.

In the beginning, we had some difficulty tuning the mast, which is stepped through the deck. We couldn't keep it straight athwartships. After taking some careful measurements, we found the massive fiberglass step to be very slightly off center. The fault was corrected by adding a little to one side of the tongue at the heel of the mast while cutting away a bit of the tongue on the other side. This completely solved the problem, and the mast is now straight as an arrow. We still have a minor difficulty with keeping the step dry because of rain entering halyard exits and running down the inside of the mast.

With the exception of not having a lightning ground system and having a companionway sill that could be slightly higher, there is not much more that's wrong with the O-38. In more than three years of testing our boat in every kind of condition from hard-driving races to a lengthy gale at sea, I've come to the conclusion that she is an exceptional all-around boat. In the words of my cousin, a veteran sailor, who sailed his first race with us last summer: "She is the sweetest boat I have ever sailed—forgiving, delicate, powerful, sure." Let us hope that the almighty rule makers will give us handicap systems that once again will encourage the production of handsome all-purpose boats that are easy to sail . . . and a pleasure . . . such as the Ohlson 38.

3

BOAT MODIFICATIONS
AND PREPARATIONS
or
"Assume That One Day the Boat
Will Turn Upside Down"

The first modification made to our Ohlson sloop was to change her name. Although doing this is supposed to bring bad luck, the boat's name had been changed previously, from *Moxie* to *Mandalay,* and I rationalized that the gods had already been offended and would not waste further displeasure on another change. We decided on *Kelpie,* the name given to three of our previous boats. A kelpie is a legendary Scottish water sprite, usually of equine form, and, incidentally, there was an infamous opium clipper of that name. According to the legend, kelpies cause and rejoice in drownings; however, they are flattered and their wrath is appeased when vessels are named after them. Thus the crews of these craft are said to be protected. At any rate, the change in name made us feel that the boat was truly ours and that she was starting a brand new life, or at least a new episode in her life.

Other modifications, of course, had to do with tuning the boat and making her ready for sea. The following is a list of changes or additions that we made (it does not include non-permanent safety equipment and the like, which will be included in the next chapter).

• Two jib sheet cleats added within reach of the helm. There should be ample cleats, and I think it is important that all sheets can be reached by the helmsman when a boat will be sailed shorthanded.

• A bilge pump, diaphragm-type Whale, installed on deck next to the helm with the discharge line looped high and the outlet through the transom. We already had one of these pumps permanently installed below. Having two greatly increases the capacity for water removal. The one on deck allows the helmsman to pump, even while steering, and the one below allows pumping when lying ahull with no one on deck.

• A removable fence installed to protect the steering quadrant. The purpose is to prevent gear stowed in the lazarette from falling and possibly jamming the quadrant.

• The engine starter button and electric fuel pump switch moved inside the companionway. I had heard of cases where the engine's starting motor shorted out because of the cockpit's filling with water that leaked through the starter button, so we changed to a system in which the cockpit button was temporarily disconnected.

• The lazarette hatch fitted with a means of securing. (This was simply a line running from an eye on the inside of the hatch to an eye at the bottom of the lazarette and thence to a cleat just inside the starboard cockpit seat locker, whose hatch is fitted with dogs and a lock.) Such an arrangement is important for safety in heavy weather, of course, and for security in port.

• An engine exhaust shut-off valve installed where the pipe goes through the transom to prevent water from entering the exhaust port and possibly finding its way into the engine's manifold during heavy weather.

• A lightning ground system installed. The system devised by Buzz White, manager of the Gibson Island Yacht Yard, with my

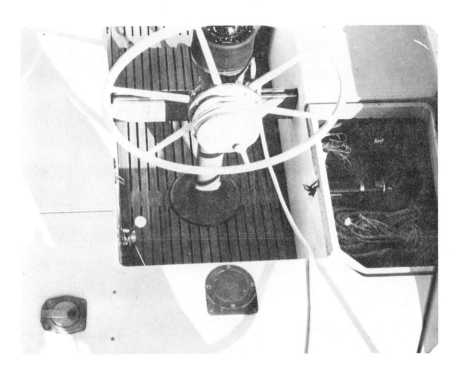

The after end of **Kelpie's** *cockpit. The dark object near the left hand corner of the well is the bilge pump (with handle unshipped) and the dark object directly abaft the wheel is the access plate for the rudder stock head to which an emergency tiller can be fitted. The open hatch at the right contains a fire extinguisher and shelf for any object the helmsman might need.*

collaboration was probably not the best, but we felt it was acceptable for *Kelpie*. The upper shrouds, stays, mast, and heating stove (near the mast) were bonded to the encased keel ballast, which had a large, exposed bolt at the bottom of the keel. A better method would have used a ground plate, but we decided against it, partly because I wanted the smoothest possible bottom for racing. With our system, we risk having a chunk of fiberglass blown off the keel, but Buzz and I feel that even if this should happen, the hull would remain watertight. I hope we are right. One can never say for sure where lightning is concerned.

• New vinyl windows and reinforcing patches in the dodger. We also attached its frame with bolts. A folding cockpit dodger is a great source of comfort and protection when sailing in exposed waters, but it must be very strong and have ample clear windows to afford good visibility.

• Two through-bolted eye straps installed on the after end of the cabin top to accept safety lines and lashings for the folded-down dodger.

• Special blocks, steering wheel drum, and other gear installed for self-steering. Details will be given in Chapter 5.

• A large block installed on the masthead crane to accept a heavy Dacron topping lift to reinforce the permanent wire lift and serve as a spare halyard. We considered installing a gallows frame for the main boom, but decided against it due to the expense, complication, and the fact that it would cause some windage and obstruct visibility to a minor extent. *Kelpie* has a rather short main boom, and we never regretted not having the gallows.

• A toggle installed aloft on the headstay to alleviate fatigue on the upper terminal fitting. Of course, the lower ends of all shrouds and stays should have toggles, and it is a good idea to add one to the upper end of the backstay if a riding sail will be carried on that stay.

• A helmsman's awning for shade on sunny days. One great advantage of having a short main boom is that it provides space between the boom end and the permanent backstay in which an awning can be hung. Sally made the awning of heavy Acrilan, and I put in many grommets around the edges and made the forward end supports, which are merely heavy poles that lashed to a pair of lifeline stanchions. The after end of the awning has a horizontal pole that slides through the cloth and lashes to the backstay. The beauty of such a shade is that it does not obstruct the helmsman's view of the sails, and the boom clears it when tacking or jibing. The awning also doubles as a collision mat.

• A fitted helmsman's folding chair. This is a modified, standard, short-legged, aluminum and canvas chair that can be folded up and stowed in the lazarette when not in use. I bolted a piece of wood across the bottom of the front legs that was

The helmsman's awning for hot weather. It is well clear of the main boom and permits an unobstructed view of the sails from the helm.

The helmsman's fairweather folding chair now pushed back for relaxing on the fantail while the boat steers herself. The white object near the horseshoe buoy is the float for the manoverboard pole.

shaped to straddle the after end of the cockpit well. The chair was a great success on our trip, but it can only be used in fair weather, of course, and it is not sufficiently robust for prolonged hard use. The aluminum legs broke during *Kelpie*'s trip home.

Rip at the helm. The weather cloth behind him affords good protection against spray coming over the windward side.

• Weather cloths (or spray dodgers, as the British often call them) to protect the cockpit from spray. They must extend far forward of the cockpit, however, to afford protection when beating to windward. Our cloths were made of dark green Acrilan.

• Storm slides for the companionway. These are in two pieces of heavy teak. The lower slide is solid (without holes) and is sufficiently high that if the cockpit should fill to the brim, water would flow over the coamings before it could flow down the companionway. The upper slide meets the horizontal sliding hatch and completely closes in the companionway. A small window in the upper slide is covered with a piece of plexiglass, which is hinged outward to allow handing things to the helmsman from below. A bar bolt prevents the lower slide from being lifted out by a boarding sea.

• Two new lockers below. These were not made because we did not have enough lockers; they were added as a result of opening

The storm slides inserted. The upper slide has a small, outward-swinging window of plexiglass for visibility and to allow passing the helmsman anything he might need desperately, such ·as the bottle of gin being passed through the window.

up sealed-off dead spaces. I like to be able to get at every part of the hull shell (for inspections, accessibility to piping, etc.), and there were areas under the stove and behind the icebox that could not be reached. We cut openings, fitted them with doors, and thus had two new lockers.

• A bulkhead-mounted, gimballed, kerosine cabin lamp for some light and even a bit of warmth without draining the batteries.

• Fiddles improved on the fore-and-aft bookshelf and the dining table. The latter's fiddles were made so that they could be removed and used with the drop leaves folded up or down. For the bookshelf over the navigation table, I made a removable fiddle held in place with shock cord as shown in Figure 3-1. Notice the piece of shock cord that runs behind the books to hold them tightly no matter how many are removed. The knot in the shock cord (on the right hand side) might not be needed if there is a keyhole slot into which the shock cord can be jammed to control tension on the cord. Net or line fiddles were added to all shelves that contained clothes or other soft gear.

• A new bookshelf added to the main bulkhead. We decided to take plenty of reading material. I never counted the books we took, but one of the crew who brought *Kelpie* home counted 75 "readable" books; presumably this did not include the many navigation manuals and tables.

• Two heavy drawers secured with drop pins as shown in Figure 3-2 to prevent them from falling out (possibly on someone's foot) when they are being opened.

• The sliding pilot berth converted to a stowage area. A special box was built to house the chronometer and sextant securely at the after end of the berth near the navigator's table. More will be said about this in Chapter 9.

• The sliding transom berth made more secure and made to lock fully out, fully in, or in an intermediate position. This arrangement enables us to vary the bunk's width for best possible comfort and security when sitting, sleeping in smooth water, or sleeping in heavy weather. Aside from this, the in positions alleviate blocking the fore-and-aft passageway.

• Lee cloths for all bunks where needed. These consist of rectangular pieces of Dacron about four feet long and a foot and a half high with grommets in the top and bottom edges. The bottom edges were lashed to beams supporting the bunk bottoms, while the top edges were lashed up with at least three lines per cloth to the overhead hand rails. This arrangement makes it all but impossible to be thrown out of a bunk; yet the cloths can be lowered quite easily in fair weather and be tucked out of the way under the mattresses by disengaging snap hooks that secure the top edges of the cloths to the overhead lines.

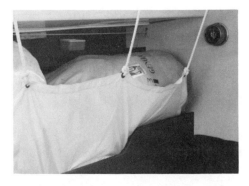

The lee cloth for Rip's pilot berth shown here ignominiously supporting a bunk full of racing sails.

FIGURE 3-1: FORE-AND-AFT BOOKSHELF

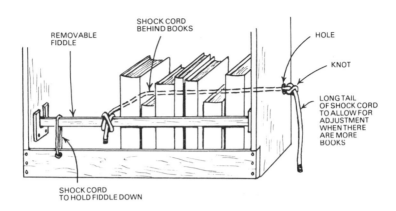

REMOVABLE
FIDDLE

SHOCK CORD
BEHIND BOOKS

HOLE

KNOT

LONG TAIL
OF SHOCK CORD
TO ALLOW FOR
ADJUSTMENT
WHEN THERE
ARE MORE
BOOKS

SHOCK CORD
TO HOLD FIDDLE DOWN

FIGURE 3-2: A SAFETIED DRAWER

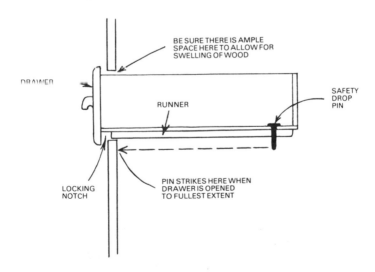

DRAWER

BE SURE THERE IS AMPLE
SPACE HERE TO ALLOW FOR
SWELLING OF WOOD

RUNNER

SAFETY
DROP
PIN

LOCKING
NOTCH

PIN STRIKES HERE WHEN
DRAWER IS OPENED
TO FULLEST EXTENT

• A cloth side curtain for the quarterberth to protect against possible spray coming down the companionway when the cockpit dodger is folded down. Another purpose is to block off light to improve sleeping conditions in the berth. The curtain was made so that it can be held back out of the way with a sash when not in use.

• A filler piece with polyurethane mattress to fill in the dinette area without the need of moving the cabin table. This gives us a comfortable if slightly-too-wide bunk, and the table's folded-down drop leaf makes a good bunk board. The table's supporting post was more securely attached to the bilge with fiberglass for extra strength. This was done by the Henry R. Hinckley Co. in Maine.

• Through-bolted eyes and safety belts for the cook and also for the person working at the navigation table while standing up. During the spring of 1975, John Letcher, the well-known designer and offshore sailor, came aboard *Kelpie* and criticized the cooking belt because it merely prevented the cook from being thrown away from, but not against, the stove. After that, we changed the design so that the belt now has two straps, back and front, to hold the cook steady no matter what the motion or angle of heel.

• An extra semi-bulkhead added under the forward bunks. Although *Kelpie* has numerous longitudinal stringers to stiffen the hull (Chapter 2), an offshore boat takes a terrific battering under the bow when encountering head seas day after day; so the bulkhead was added to assure stiffness in that most vulnerable area. I had written to the Tyler Boat Company (*Kelpie*'s molder) explaining our intentions and asking for advice on any modifications they might think necessary. They answered that in their opinion the boat needed little modification but suggested a thorough examination of the through-hull fittings and the possible addition of the bulkhead, depending on just how *Kelpie* was finished (she was completed in Ohlson's yard). I also asked Tyler's opinion about glassing over the inside of the hollow skeg (to maintain watertightness in the event it should break), but they felt this was unnecessary, since this skeg is very shallow and strong and has a wide flaring base attaching it to the hull.

• Propeller changed before the ocean passage. We changed from a 14-inch-diameter Michigan with folding blades to a 16-inch prop with solid blades. I figured the larger solid prop would be more reliable and efficient under power, but now I feel the change was not worthwhile because of the small amount of time the engine was run and the extra drag the solid blades caused when we were under sail.

In addition to the above modifications, of course, there was much existing unmodified gear that needed thorough inspecting and servicing. For instance, the rig and all related fittings were examined aloft and alow. I painted most of the swaged terminal fittings with Magnaflux dye and penetrant and examined them with a magnifying glass to look for microscopic cracks that could lead to possible fitting failures. Also, the rigging wire was given a careful going-over to look for corrosion or broken strands, especially where the wires enter the terminal sockets (a usual place where failures occur). The spreaders, too, got a lot of attention, because failure of these can lead to loss of the mast. We wrapped the tips in soft felt to minimize chafe on the head-sails but later used Tingley rubber boots, which seemed to work very well. I cut short lengths of clear vinyl hose to serve as turnbuckle boots. They allow examination of the turnbuckles and cotter pins.

The winches (two No. 22 Barients, two No. 28 Barients, a No. 24 Barient reel, and a small, top-action Merriman) were dismantled, cleaned, and lubricated. In addition, the worm-screw outhaul fitting and roller reefing gear were well greased. The steering cable was also lubricated and carefully examined for broken strands.

Especially well inspected were the shut-off valves for the through-hull fittings, because most of them were gate valves, which are often inferior to seacocks (barrel-plug valves that operate with handles). In *Kelpie*'s case, however, the valves were a superior solid-ball type made of high-quality bronze rather than brass, and they proved to be in excellent shape. Hoses and piping were checked, and many hose clamps were replaced and extras added wherever possible. Of course, the yard mechanic checked over the engine including all fuel lines, filters, and controls. The toilet was dismantled and several worn parts (check valve, spring, and gasket) were replaced.

Buzz White checked over most of the wiring and the navigation lights and spreader lights. He also examined the most-important binnacle light, renewed the rubber compass mounts, and replaced some badly corroded brass screws in the binnacle with ones made of non-magnetic stainless steel.

Other vital checks were those of the life line assembly, galley stove, and windows. New lashings were put on the upper life lines (the lowers had pelican hooks), and nets were rigged forward, between the pulpit and bow stanchions, to prevent lowered headsails from washing overboard. The HilleRange, three-burner, alcohol stove was thoroughly cleaned, touched up with rustoleum where needed, and its gimballing was increased to about 35 degrees both ways. Also, a couple of standard pot holders were fitted to its sea rails. The plexiglass windows were taken out of their frames to see if they were sufficiently thick and to renew the bedding. Buzz and I decided that storm shutters would be unnecessary due to the small window area and adequate thickness of plexiglass. Underwater checks made after *Kelpie* was hauled included inspection of the rudder (especially the heel fitting), rudder and prop bearings, sacrificial zincs (to prevent galvanic corrosion), fathometer transducer, and speed-ometer sensor.

As thorough as the above checks may seem, they were not entirely adequate, because we later found that the ports needed new gaskets, there was a hidden flaw in the engine's exhaust line, and water leaked through the rudder stock when the stern pounded in heavy weather. Although the propeller shaft stuffing box had been repacked, the gland on the rudder stock was over-looked due to the fact that it had given no trouble during a year of hard sailing on the Chesapeake Bay. These and a few more oversights or miscalculations will be discussed in the last chapter.

Of course most of the major work was done by Buzz White and the Gibson Island yard, and a splendid job they did, but I attended to many of the smaller tasks, and it was most pleasant pottering about the boat during the spring of 1975. In May, Rip was able to join me, and one of the good jobs he did was to sand and oil all the teak brightwork. I spent a great deal of time installing eye straps down below for rope fiddles, belts (made by Sally), and lashings. Very often gear is spilled in heavy weather, and I was determined that everything would stay in place on *Kelpie.* Even the storm anchor, carried under the forward bunks, was securely lashed in place. I recalled the words of the famous circumnavigator, Edward Allcard, when he said, "Assume that one day the boat will turn upside down." There was not much chance of that, really, but it is wise and comforting to be prepared for any eventuality.

4

SAFETY AND MEDICAL
CONSIDERATIONS
or
All Our Eggs in One Basket

Kelpie's ocean cruise was a very literal example of putting all our eggs in one basket. Committed to our woven glass coracle was every member of our immediate family; therefore, we weren't about to shirk on what we considered was proper safety equipment.

First and foremost was the life raft, for that is to the ocean sailor what a parachute is to the flyer. Of course, not everyone agrees that a raft is vital, but more than a few good boats have foundered from collisions with ships, flotsam, or whales; unusual weather; or some other cause. A solid dinghy or even an inflatable boat that has no canopy and can easily capsize will not afford the same degree of safety as a proper raft.

After much research, including talking to life raft inspectors and corresponding with *The Telltale Compass* (a kind of consumer's report for yachtsmen), we decided on a six-man, Elliot "Sea-Jay" raft made by the C. J. Hendry Company of San Francisco. I remember Sally's question when we visited the office of a prominent raft inspector, who was said to be the most experienced in the port of Baltimore. She looked at a photograph of the man's wife and children on his desk and asked him what make of raft he would want for his own family, price being no object. Without hesitation the inspector replied, "an Elliot."

The Sea-Jay is built to Coast Guard standards and is recommended by Survival and Safety Designs, marine survival authorities and suppliers (P.O. Box 562, Alameda, California 94501). Although there are other good makes, Avon and Swiklik for example, none but the Elliot (at the time of our purchase, at least) had as high a degree of quality combined with all the important safety features. For instance, the highly touted standard Avon, in contrast with the Elliot, had no air chamber under the bottom for wave protection and insulation. I was interested to hear from Maurice Bailey, who with his wife, Maralyn, spent 118 days in an Avon after their boat had been sunk by a whale, that he felt this air chamber was extremely important, and he now carries a custom-made Avon with the chamber included. In addition, we heard from inspectors that the Avon's fiberglass cannister is not as sturdy nor as well-sealed as the Elliot's, and when water penetrates the cannister, the raft and equipment can deteriorate.

Another point in favor of the Elliot, we think, is that our model is somewhat boat-shaped and can be provided with a sail for propulsion downwind. Other rafts that are round and are not intended for locomotion lack the advantage of being able to reach a nearby shore or steamer lane. Although the round rafts may have a more stable shape, especially the deep-bottom, water-ballasted type, such as the Givens raft, the Elliot is provided with four effective water pockets on the bottom to inhibit capsizing greatly, and it will not spin like the circular types.

Some other features of our raft are: two arch tubes to support the canopy; an arrangement for water catchment; two lights, one inside the canopy and one exterior automatic beacon; supplies sealed in waterproof nylon; interior lifeline and rough-water safety strap; rugged painter/tow line attachment point; safety knife (with round tip) mounted in a handy location to cut the painter; a large drogue that ejects automatically; exterior safety lines; heaving line; boarding ladder; and, of course, double buoyancy tubes, either one being capable of supporting the fully-loaded raft in a level position.

One feature that worried me a little, probably needlessly, was the thin diameter of the raft's painter, which is pulled to open the valve of the CO_2 bottle, thereby inflating the raft. Of course, there is a reason for having such a light line: The end of it is attached to the vessel, and if the sinking should happen very suddenly, before the raft could be inflated, the sinking vessel's pull on the line would cause inflation and then parting of the painter. Obviously, the line cannot be too heavy or it might not break, and the raft would then go down with the ship. Nevertheless, I was somewhat concerned that during a slow sinking, after the cannister had been thrown overboard, the line might be pulled against a sharp object such as the rail track, which could possibly cut the painter, allowing the raft to drift away before it could be boarded. Such an accident would seem very unlikely, but I had heard of it happening during the abandoning of the powerboat *Fancy Free* in 1968.

An optional feature we did not have, by the way, was a hydrostatic release. This is a device that releases the cannister automatically when it is about fifteen feet under water in the event the vessel should sink very suddenly before the raft can be released from its secured position on deck.

The raft inspectors and some other authorities convinced us that having our raft sealed in a sturdy fiberglass cannister that could be secured on deck was the only way to go (for speed of launching and raft protection). But we had a problem in decid-ing where to secure the cannister. There was space on the after deck, but in that location the cannister would interfere with opening the lazarette hatch, and also I did not want that much weight (115 pounds) on the stern.

Clare Francis carried her raft (aboard the O-38 *Robertson's Golly*) on the cabin top just forward of the mainmast. We considered that, and there was a perfect space there where the raft would not interfere with the opening of the forward hatch, but the location was quite exposed, and I foresaw the possibility of green water coming aboard and breaking loose the cannister. Furthermore, it would obstruct our working at the mast when handing or hoisting sails. Although the cannister is sturdy enough to stand on, it is somewhat slippery, and it is held closed by metal bands that we thought could be broken accidentally. The bands are designed to part with the pressure of the raft being inflated, thus it seemed conceivable that a hard kick from a sailhandler's foot could cause an accidental parting. Then too, the gasket seal could be damaged by constantly standing on the cannister.

We finally decided, after talking the matter over with a raft inspector, that we'd secure the cannister under the overturned dinghy. This is not supposed to be the safest practice, because the dinghy blocks accessibility to the raft, but we secured the dink with snap shackles so that it could be released in a matter of seconds. Advantages of the raft's location were that it would

Kelpie's fiberglass dinghy, a Dyer dhow, is shown upside down on the cabin top. It is secured with snapshackles that have lanyards on their pull pins to assure instant release. The picture also shows such details as the foredeck nets, clear turnbuckle boots, and double gates on the mainsail track with the storm trysail bent on.

be in a secure place where it could not be torn loose in heavy weather, and it kept the weight amidships. In the event we had to abandon *Kelpie,* we wanted to take the dinghy as well as the raft; so we didn't think there was a great disadvantage in stowing both in the same location, provided the dink could be released immediately for accessibility to the raft.

Our Elliot was equipped with a standard ocean pack that included such items as: paddles; inflation pump; bilge pump; leak stopper clamps; repair kit; floating sheath knife; survival manual; boarding and righting instructions; sponges; bailer; waterproof flashlight with spare batteries and bulb; whistle; flares; parachute signals; signal mirror; first aid kit; seasickness pills; canned food and water; graduated drinking cup; and can openers. In addition, of course, we had other supplies handy such as extra food and water, a small strobe light, freon horn, dye marker, emergency radio, and navigation kit.

The latter is surplus from World War II and contains a plastic sextant, instruction book with tables and star chart, plotting sheets, dividers, pencils, protractor, etc. Of course, if forced to abandon ship, we would also have taken my Timex watch, the current Nautical or Air Almanac, and the good sextant, if we had had time to grab it.

Speaking of life raft supplies, I was amused when not long before our trip some friends tested a Winslow raft, a cheaper popular make that has been harshly criticized by many authorities. The particular raft being tested had a number of deficiencies, including only half as much CO_2 as was needed for full inflation. Among the inadequate emergency gear was a large bottle of insect repellent, which I suppose would come in very handy if one were shipwrecked on the upper reaches of the Amazon. But at sea? I'd far rather have an extra can of water. As said before, the Winslow is relatively cheap, and one usually gets what he pays for. Our Elliot, however, was not really that much more expensive, for it cost $1,196 (in December, 1974), and the price included the fiberglass cannister and ocean emergency gear. Furthermore, we were assured that the Elliots had good resale value.

For emergency communications, we had two portable transmitting radios. One was a small Narco EPIRB (emergency position indicating radio beacon) made by Narco Marine, Fort Washington, Pennsylvania 19034. This transmits a distress signal on the aviation emergency frequencies 121.5 and 243 MHz. I didn't feel the Narco was all we needed, however, despite its long range of up to 200 miles in all directions (according to advertisements), because it does not broadcast on the international marine distress frequency of 2182 KHz. For this purpose, we had a British Callbuoy (made by Callbuoy Marine Electronics, 6 Somerset Road, Cumbran, Gwent, Wales) that can broadcast either an alarm signal or voice. In effect, it is a portable radiotelephone that allows one to make safety and urgency calls as well as distress calls. The drawback of the Callbuoy is that its range is relatively short (about 45 miles or more). Nevertheless, it can be used to call nearby ships, and I was interested to learn that Maurice Bailey, mentioned earlier, carries a Callbuoy on his new boat.

Some people have asked why we carried no permanently installed single sideband and/or VHF radios. The answer is that the latter has a very short range while the former is quite expensive. More important than these factors, however, is the way these radios change the aspect of an ocean cruise. One does not get the complete satisfaction through a feeling of independence and self-reliance when he has the ability to make conversation with the outside world at any time. All we wanted was the ability to call for help in the event of a serious emergency. Another important safety consideration is that our portable equipment could be carried with us in the raft, while permanent equipment would go down with the ship if she should happen to founder.

At this point, I can't resist telling my favorite story about emergency communications. The owner of a large powerboat got into some trouble and called the Coast Guard on his radiotelephone. The C.G. asked, "What is your position?" There was a pause, and then the reply came back: "Well, I'm vice president of the so-and-so company."

Other means of communication on *Kelpie* were: a complete set of signal flags, a battery-powered loud-hailer with horn, signal light, and flares. The signal light was a 22,000-candle-power Guest Signal/Sail powered by its own six-volt battery and having a spring-loaded switch for Morse code. It also doubled as a powerful waterproof spotlight. As for flares, we carried red parachute and meteors together with a modern flare gun and an old-fashioned Very pistol (more will be said about this in the next chapter). In addition, we had plenty of white and red hand-held flares and a number of hand-held orange smoke flares for daytime use.

Of course *Kelpie* was equipped with adequate Coast Guard approved PFDs (personal flotation devices), and also a horseshoe buoy was hung on the stern pulpit where it could be thrown overboard immediately if someone should happen to go over the side. Attached to the horseshoe was a Guest xenon strobe flashing light that goes on automatically when it rights itself after being thrown in the water. Also attached to the horseshoe was an eight-foot fiberglass man-overboard pole made by Ratsey and Lapthorn. The pole was attached to the permanent backstay by inserting its top end (to which an orange flag was fastened) through a plastic cylinder lashed to the backstay, while its bottom, ballasted end rested on the deck after being inserted into a loose rope ring. To release the pole, the bottom is lifted out of the rope ring, and then the top can easily be pulled out of its cylinder so that the pole and horseshoe can be thrown overboard in the quickest possible time.

Aside from these man-overboard devices, we had one flotation jacket from L. L. Bean of Freeport, Maine, that could be worn by any of us, and it was mandatory equipment for the helmsman at night. The jacket is bright orange for good visibility. It is warm and comfortable and has a sturdy, easy-to-manage zipper, but it has one possible deficiency: no leg straps to hold it down. We didn't test the jacket, but I heard from a friend, who had occasion to use one after a capsizing, that it rode up around his face and that it needs a strap or straps passing between the legs to hold it down. Our jacket has slash pockets (although I would prefer flap types), and in one of them we always carried a signal whistle and small strobe flasher (ours was made by Neo-Flasher Electronics of Hollywood, California).

Another piece of equipment worn by the helmsman at night was a safety belt. We had four harness types with sturdy safety lines and stainless steel snap hooks for attachment to the rigging or elsewhere. The snap hooks were the interlocking type used by mountain climbers that can be opened and closed very easily, yet the hook cannot be bent upward after the snap has been closed. Rip and I always wore a safety belt in heavy weather when going forward to change a sail, and we had Sally to thank for insisting that we do so in marginal conditions. *Kelpie* was fitted with bright-colored Dacron jacklines running from eyes on either side of the companionway to the mast on both the port and starboard sides, so that a person could clip on his safety line's snap hook at the cockpit and go forward without having to unclip. The jacklines allowed uninterrupted fore-and-aft travel.

One recognized hazard in going to sea in a small boat is the chance of being run down by a ship or fishing vessel when there is poor visibility. Actually, the risk is slight, but the possibility exists. We have a seagoing friend who was run down twice. An important safeguard against such accidents is a proper radar reflector, and in my opinion, the size of the reflector should be inversely proportional to the size of the boat. One often sees very small boats with tiny reflectors, but they should have large ones. Ours was medium-sized, an approximately two-by-two-foot octahedral type (with eight corners) made of light metal. There is usually a problem as to where to carry the reflector. Many times it is hoisted to a spreader, but there it is apt to chafe the mainsail when the boom is broad off. We mounted ours high on the permanent backstay. This was possible because of the short main boom, which left a lot of space between the mainsail's leech and the backstay. A small block to support a halyard by which the reflector could be hoisted was clamped to the backstay with compression sleeves. A downhaul held the reflector steady and there was a short safety wire shackled to the back-

An ocean sailing scene with dramatic lighting on the radar reflector. The backstay location is a good one provided the reflector can be hoisted to a height of at least 12 feet. Here it cannot chafe the sails or foul the halyards. Orientation of the reflector would be better with a three-point suspension, but this is more difficult to achieve.

stay so that if the halyard should happen to chafe through, the reflector would not fall on the helmsman's head but would merely slide down the backstay.

Another safeguard against being run down is a powerful flare-up light. Some boats now carry masthead-mounted strobe lights, and we gave such a light consideration but didn't think it necessary, because *Kelpie* has adequate spreader lights that illuminate the sails and deck. Also we carried white flares near the companionway, and, of course, we had the strobe flasher attached to the horseshoe buoy within easy reach of the helmsman. As a matter of fact, flashing strobe lights should be used with caution, because they can attract ships rather than cause them to turn away. A flasher should probably not be used except in extremis, when collision seems almost imminent.

For fire fighting we had three dry chemical BC-1 (Coast Guard classification) extinguishers, one mounted forward, one in the main cabin opposite the galley, and a third on deck under a cockpit seat locker. I feel that *Kelpie* is safe with respect to fire, because she carries no gasoline or L.P. gas for cooking. The only explosive substance we carried was a small aerosol can of engine starting booster containing ether, which can be sprayed (with great restraint) into the engine's air intake in the event that starting should be difficult. The can was stowed forward, far away from the galley and engine. Incidentally, to conserve our batteries, we usually started the engine with its compression levers up. Once the fly wheel was spinning, the levers would be put down to restore compression, and then the engine would fire up immediately.

About the only real danger of fire came from our alcohol stove, but of course alcohol fires can be extinguished with water, provided enough is used to prevent smoldering. A few boats have been lost from alcohol fires as a result of smoldering after the fires were thought to be extinguished or else as a result of not being able to reach the shut-off valve because of its being surrounded by flames. On *Kelpie* we had a remote shut-off far away from the stove where flames could not reach it.

Medical supplies and first aid procedures should get very careful consideration when planning a long ocean passage, because doctors are hard to find at sea, and obviously the offshore sailor cannot run down to the corner drug store for medicines. We were very fortunate to have a number of doctor friends who gave us considerable help with our preparations. Especially helpful were the wife-husband doctor team Anne and Dennis Wentz. Both of them are enthusiastic sailors, and they were tremendously interested in our trip. Not only did they suggest supplies and medicines, but they supplied much of the equipment and many of the drugs, and gave us rudimentary training in advanced first aid. I remember one evening sitting in our living room suturing and giving injections to grapefruits. We were told that grapefruit rind is good to practice on, because in certain respects it resembles human flesh. At the end of that evening I resolved that we would all be extra careful in mid-Atlantic.

Our first aid kits consisted of a large plastic fishing box and Tupperware bucket with a tight-fitting top. They contained such equipment as: a scalpel with disposable blades; Halsted clamp; Kelly clamp; two I.V. (intravenous) bags with administration sets; a catheter tube; a packet of wood cotton-tipped applicators; a pair of disposable latex surgeon's gloves; surgical scissors; forceps; surgical needles with gut thread; packaged sterile hypodermic syringes; airway resuscitube; arch wire fracture splint; air splints; ear applicator; sponges; post-operative dressings; Dermicel surgical tape; Vaseline petroleum gauze dressings; compress gauze; elastic bandages; and numerous other bandages and dressings, including, of course, the ubiquitous Band-Aid.

Dennis brought two young pharmacists, who were interested in our trip, down to Gibson Island to look over our boat. They brought with them most of our drugs and medications with written directions for usage. Our medicines, mostly requiring prescriptions, included: Bucladin and Meclizine Hydrochloride (Bonine), for seasickness; Benadryl, an antiemetic (for seasickness) and antihistamine as well; Compazine tablets, injection, and suppositories, for management of severe nausea and vomiting; Donnatal tablets, for gastro-intestinal problems (spasms, nausea, vomiting, gastritis, hyperacidity, nervous indigestion, spastic or irritable colon, and spastic constipation); Lomotil tablets, for extreme diarrhea; Robitussin A-C, for suppression of coughing; Afrin 0.05% nasal solution, for relief of nasal congestion; Tinactin 1% solution, for athlete's foot (fungus); Dexamethasone, for severe sunburn; Pyridium tablets, for relief of burning, urgency, or other discomforts from irritation of the lower urinary tract; Keflex capsules (antibiotic), for severe urinary tract and upper respiratory infections; Potassium Phenoxymethyl Penicillin tablets (antibiotic), for respiratory

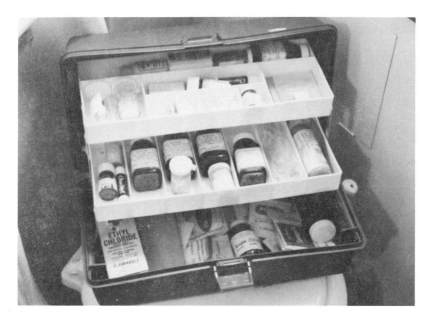

The plastic fishing box that held our numerous medicines and first aid supplies.

tract, strep throat, pneumonia, and skin infections; Terramycin salve (antibiotic), for minor abrasions and skin infections; Lactinex, for replenishment of normal bacteria to the colon after diarrhea; Dexedrine (amphetamine sulfate), for staying awake when necessary (hallucinations might occur with exhaustion; should not be taken concomitantly with alcohol); Seconal capsules, for insomnia and sedation (should not be taken concomitantly with alcohol); Dilaudid tablets, for relief of severe pain (should not be taken concomitantly with alcohol); Codeine sulfate tablets, for relief of mild to moderate pain (should not be taken concomitantly with alcohol); Xylocaine, local anesthetic; Ethyl Chloride spray, local anesthetic; Ophthaine solution, an anesthetic for removal of foreign objects from the eye; Chloromycetin, eye ointment; Otodyne, ear drops; Sudafed, for sinus infection; Metamucil, for constipation; Mycostatin vaginal inserts (antifungal suppositories), for relief of itching; Sultrin vaginal cream, for relief of itching; Betadine solution (antiseptic), for skin sterilization; and Desitin ointment, for sore bottoms from excessive sitting on hard decks (sometimes called "fiberglarse").

Fortunately, we did not have to use any of these medications, except occasionally the Bonine for seasickness and the Tinactin for athlete's foot. However, Sally dispensed the Mycostatin to a stricken female sailor in the Azores. Apparently, although it is seldom mentioned, vaginal itch is not unusual among female voyagers, from sitting around in wet clothing. Any woman who plans a long cruise should consult her gynecologist. As a matter of fact, it makes good sense for either sex to have a thorough physical examination before embarking on a long offshore passage.

A word of warning about our list of medical supplies: Anyone contemplating a voyage should certainly not consider this list as final. Some doctors might disagree with it or think there should be more or different items. Furthermore, I have given no details of the medicines or directions for taking them or their side effects and possible adverse reactions. The list is merely intended as a starting point in medical preparation. The prospective voyager should by all means consult with his own doctor. Of course, a good first aid manual is vital and some that are intended for mariners contain good lists of medical supplies. Our principal manual, considered one of the best, was *Advanced First Aid Afloat,* written by Dr. Peter F. Eastman. Another good book is Dr. Paul B. Sheldon's *First Aid Afloat.*

Naturally, we carried other medically related supplies such as aspirin and sun screens (we used PreSun), but these are the kind of items that are normally found on every cruising boat, so I won't waste a page by listing them all. As said before, Rip was given the job of shipboard medic, because he had shown some interest in the subject, and I am a bit squeamish at the sight of blood (my own especially). We felt that Rip prepared himself for the job quite well, as he spent a day or so in the emergency room of a hospital watching accident victims being sewn up and treated for various ailments.

The medical aspect of our cruise brought home in still another way the value of preparing for even a minor endeavor such as ours. The voyager delves into a great variety of subjects during his preparations, and he learns a little about many things that otherwise he might never come to know, were it not for his realization of the need for total self-sufficiency.

5

ANCILLARY AND EXTRA GEAR
or
Blackbeard Beware

Aside from the safety and medical equipment discussed in the last chapter, a long passage offshore requires many extra supplies, numerous spares, and some unusual gear not normally found on a coastwise cruiser. The most thorough preparations must consider every possible need, and there should be a plan for every conceivable contingency.

One piece of gear on which Buzz White and I put considerable thought was an emergency steering system. Breakdowns of primary systems are becoming so common that jury methods of steering are being required on some long-distance ocean races. Of course, we always carry an emergency tiller in the event that our wheel steering should fail, but I felt we also should have an emergency rudder. The arrangement we finally decided on was one that would not require the mounting of gudgeons on the transom nor the carrying of an extra bulky rudder blade. For the latter we used the removable engine compartment door, a sturdy piece of plywood composed of nine laminations, and we drilled holes in it to accept bolts that would secure it to the rudder stock. Jim Potter, a fine craftsman at the yacht yard, made the stock from a heavy steel rod. It fit through a hollow pipe that could be secured with a number of hose clamps to the stern pulpit. Buzz and I felt the pulpit was strong enough to support the emergency rudder, because it had four sturdy legs, two of them being through-bolted to the deck and the other two being secured to the heavy stern rail with eight long screws.

The emergency rudder. The plywood engine compartment door that serves as the rudder blade is shown bolted to the rudder stock.

Detail of the emergency rudder stock head with the steering yoke that will accept steering lines leading to the wheel drum.

Furthermore, the bottom of the rudder stock would be held with support lines as shown in Figure 5-1. At the top of the stock there was a cross bar for steering lines. The bottom of the stock was filed flat, drilled for the rudder blade bolts, and bent aft so that it could grip the blade with proper leverage (see accompanying photographs).

For self-steering, we had a QME vane gear made by Quantock Marine Enterprises of Bridgewater, Somerset, England. We had used the vane on our previous boat, which was smaller and had a tiller, so I had some doubts about the capability of the gear on the larger O-38 with her steering wheel. I had experimented with hooking the vane to the emergency tiller, but this did not work very well, so I ordered a standard steering drum that is bolted to the wheel. It is made by Marine Vane Gears of Cowes, England, for the express purpose of attaching a self-steering gear to a wheel (see Figure 5-2). This enabled the QME to work quite well, at least when the wind was forward of the beam. More will be said about how we made *Kelpie* steer herself in Chapter 8.

The QME is a very simple device with no underwater parts, and its vane turns on a horizontal axis (see Figure 5-3). We had to add a supporting strut to the stern, but this was easily accomplished without defacing the after deck or transom. The forward end of the strut was held by one bolt through the top of the cockpit coaming, and about three feet farther aft, the strut was held securely to a stern pulpit stanchion with "U" bolts. When not in use, the vane could be unshipped quite easily and lashed on its side to the life line stanchions. Also, the strut was quite easy to remove, although we always carried it intact during our cruise.

Our ground tackle was actually less than what we would have taken on a lengthy coastal cruise. We had a 13-pound Danforth lunch hook, a 35-pound CQR plow, and our standard working anchor, a 20-pound Hi-tensile Danforth that has held us in many a hard blow. On a long coastal cruise over rocky or weed-covered bottoms, I would take a Herreshoff yachtsman type in addition. We did take, however, two sea anchors, conic "cornu-

FIGURE 5-1: EMERGENCY RUDDER

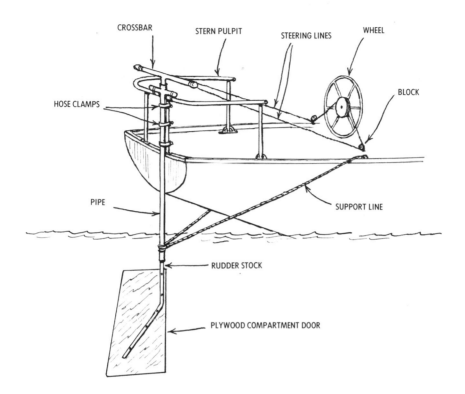

CROSSBAR

STERN PULPIT

STEERING LINES

WHEEL

BLOCK

HOSE CLAMPS

PIPE

SUPPORT LINE

RUDDER STOCK

PLYWOOD COMPARTMENT DOOR

FIGURE 5-2: DRUM FOR STEERING WHEEL

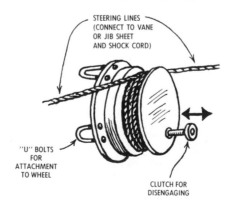

STEERING LINES
(CONNECT TO VANE
OR JIB SHEET
AND SHOCK CORD)

"U" BOLTS
FOR
ATTACHMENT
TO WHEEL

CLUTCH FOR
DISENGAGING

FIGURE 5-3: SELF-STEERING VANE

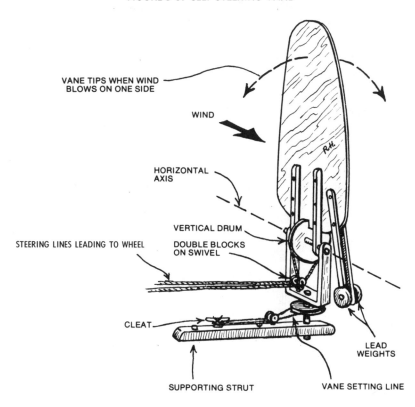

VANE TIPS WHEN WIND
BLOWS ON ONE SIDE

WIND

HORIZONTAL
AXIS

VERTICAL DRUM

STEERING LINES LEADING TO WHEEL

DOUBLE BLOCKS
ON SWIVEL

CLEAT

LEAD
WEIGHTS

SUPPORTING STRUT

VANE SETTING LINE

copia" types, and an automobile tire for use as a drag. Our standard anchor rode is 150 feet of five-eighths-inch nylon, and I got an extra 200 feet of three-quarter-inch nylon. Some cruising sailors might prefer longer rodes and heavier anchors, but I felt what we had was sufficient for our purpose with a 15,000-pound boat. Furthermore, in heavy weather I use a 30-foot chain leader that weighs 48 pounds, and this not only increases holding power but affords protection against chafe.

The tire was a small one I found on the beach at Gibson Island, and it had been so well scrubbed by sand and sea that it never left any black marks on the boat. Its primary purpose was to reduce boat speed by towing it astern in the event that heavy weather forced us to run off the wind. We never actually used the tire for a drag but seriously considered doing so, as the reader will learn later. A secondary purpose was for use as a rugged fender. We had heard that boats must be well fendered when made fast to the rough seawall at Horta, in the Azores, and elsewhere. Also, I had read that a tire makes a good sea anchor when it is towed upright from a bridle. We carried it lashed flat on the cabin top with drain holes drilled in the tire's underside. Sally objected to the looks of it, so she made an attractive form-fitting cover out of waterproof cloth. Perhaps the real reason I liked the tire was that it was the one piece of equipment I didn't have to pay for.

As the old song from World War I advised, we packed up our troubles in our old kit bag. More accurately, we packed up a lot of gear that would prevent trouble in many kit bags. There were kits of tools, a kit for sail repairs, a kit of engine spare parts, a kit for plumbing repairs, a kit for emergency signaling, a kit of electrical spares, and so forth. Some of the bags containing the kits came from West Products of Boston, but Sally made most of them herself from heavy acrylic cloth (see Chapter 6).

The engine kit included two fuel filters, two oil filters, three belts, a water pump impeller, a diaphragm kit for the main fuel pump, a spare electric fuel pump, and a small utility pump. Ample lube oil was carried in a waterproof plastic bag. A combination plumbing and leak repair kit contained a variety of hoses and hose clamps, a few spare parts for the head, flax packing, duct tape, caulking cotton, Mortite caulking cord, silicone sealer, soft putty, two-part epoxy paste, epoxy compound (Poxy Putty) that will set underwater, heavy grease (Lubriplate), and tapered plugs of soft wood that would fit every through-hull fitting. In addition, we had an extra diaphragm and flap valves for the bilge pumps. A stove kit contained a spare burner, an extra burner control handle, a special wrench, and numerous small spare parts for the kerosine stove (our stoves will be described in Chapter 11). The electrical kit included spare bulbs for all lights, spare wire, electrical tape, hydrometer for testing the main batteries, fuses, and many dry cell batteries for all radios and flashlights.

A rigging kit contained spare turnbuckles, toggles, pins, cotters, shackles, bolts, eyes, blocks, metal straps, bullseye clamps, short pieces of chain to reinforce the rigging if it should be weakened or break, binding wire, a two-foot-long stainless steel threaded rod with nuts, and so forth. An extra shroud was carried also. A combination sewing and sail repair kit contained extra hanks, sail slides, slugs, a grommet-making kit, sail tape, boat tape, Dacron cloth for patching, and of course many needles, thread, beeswax, palm, fid, marlin spike, marlin, and twine.

Incidentally, an entire shelf was reserved for the stowage of short lashing lines. There never seem to be enough of these on a boat. This deficiency was pointed out to me many years ago when my cousin Ed Henderson, formerly a regular crew member, gave me an elaborately wrapped Christmas present consisting of a single short line with whipped ends. It seems that I was always calling for a short piece, and he could never find one.

Our emergency signaling kit, of course, contained the flare gun and flares mentioned in the last chapter. In addition, the kit held an antique Very pistol, which had a double purpose. Several people had suggested that we carry a weapon for self-defense, since there had been a few recent cases of piracy, although not in the area in which we planned to cruise. On the other hand, we heard there is some risk in carrying firearms to certain foreign ports, because you could be detained by much red tape. The old Very pistol seemed a good solution, because it could be used as a weapon yet was legal as an emergency signaling device. Besides, it was such a formidable looking gun, I felt reasonably sure it would frighten away Blackbeard himself.

Although there was a drawer near the companionway that we used for small, frequently-used tools, such as pliers and screw drivers, we had several bags for large tools used less frequently. These contained a cold chisel, hacksaw and blades, saw set with interchangeable blades, hammer, hatchet, vise-grip pliers, ad-

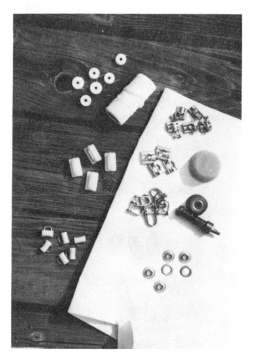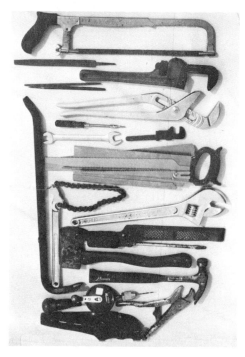

Some of the items from our tool and sewing/sail repair kits. The tools include some not-so-usual implements, such as a surform, chain wrench, and flexible screwdriver.

justable end wrenches (including a No. 16 that would fit the largest nut on the boat), a set of non-adjustable end wrenches, a socket wrench set, chain wrench, large adjustable channel pliers, Stillson wrench, monkey wrench, brace with bits and a screw driver bit, drill with assorted bits, a surform (for planing and rasping wood), gouge, wood chisels, tin snips, files, wood clamps, adjustable hose clamps ("Make-A-Clamp"), and a number of knives. Separately, we carried a large wrecking bar for prying off the wood ceiling or breaking turnbuckles, etc., and a heavy pair of rigging cutters. I had heard of difficulties in cutting 1 X 19 stainless steel rigging with some cutters; so I tested ours. The five-sixteenths-inch wire used for our rigging could not be cut on the first try, but it could be cut after two or three rapid squeezes.

Water is obviously a prime consideration for an ocean cruise. We had one 48-gallon fiberglass tank bonded in the keel. I would have preferred two tanks in case one should happen to leak or its contents should turn bad, but *Kelpie*'s tank is very well made, is adequately baffled, and had been pressure tested to three pounds per square inch. Furthermore, we had never had any problems with water turning foul in the tank, and also we planned to carry ample soft drinks, beer, and juices. Still, I thought it would be wise to take plenty of spare water; so we carried 25 gallons in nine separate containers, mostly in jerry jugs. We felt this was ample spare water because of the large quantity of other drinkable liquids we carried. Nearly all the jugs were carried tightly squeezed in and lashed into the U-shaped area under the dinette berth. This arrangement would have deprived us of leg room under the table on the port side had the dinette been in use, but at sea the settee was always converted to a berth, and we only ate from the fore and aft ends and starboard side of the table. Despite a slow passage to the Azores, we never had to use the extra water. However, Ed Karkow was glad to have it on the way home, because he didn't like the taste of the water with which we topped off the tank in Horta, although that water was perfectly pure.

Kelpie's fuel tank, also in the keel, only holds 20 gallons; we carried 17½ extra gallons in five red jerry jugs. These were carried on deck, so there would be no smell of diesel oil in the cabin, and the jugs were wedged into the cockpit well and lashed securely to the mid-cockpit traveler. They were not in the way, because the two largest jugs were fit between the traveler and binnacle where people rarely sit. A further advantage of keeping the extra fuel in the cockpit was that the jugs reduced the well's volume, thereby reducing the weight of water from a possible boarding sea that might fill the well.

One experienced cruising sailor has advised against using jerry jugs, as some of his had leaked, but we had no trouble with ours, which were made by Dillon-Beck Company, of Hillside,

New Jersey. We did develop leaks, however, in two collapsible water bags made by L. L. Bean. Probably this was due to the fact that we froze the water in the bags in order to keep our food cold for the first week at sea.

Some miscellaneous items not yet mentioned were: a spare steering cable, extra lines (including long docking lines), a 150-foot coil of half-inch Dacron line, portable piston-type bilge pump, spare winch handles (also extra pawls and springs), a handybilly tackle (in addition to the regular boom vang tackle), extra sail stops and battens, an extra pair of good 7 X 50 binoculars, a large sheet of one-inch-thick polyurethane for padding and plugging possible leaks, extra heavy-duty blocks, a fisherman's thermometer (for measuring the water temperature), a five-foot-long floating cockpit cushion (as well as many standard buoyant seat cushions), numerous flashlights (the most versatile was a Sears No. 344814 bicycle light), two kerosine riding lights (in case the main batteries should fail), a quarantine and Portuguese courtesy flag (with a halyard rigged to the star-board spreader), a proper lead line (in addition to our Seafarer fathometer), and a large junk bag (containing nails, screws, nuts, eye straps, glues, wire, etc.). Of course there was a bell for fog, and we carried a spare freon horn as well as a mouth horn. Needless to say, we had receiving radios and a lot of navigation equipment, but these will be discussed in Chapter 9.

Our barometer was augmented by a device that was facetious-ly given to us by an old friend. It consists of two glass birds that are supposed to herald changes in the weather by changing their color. When the birds are blue the weather should be fair, but if they turn pink you would do well to reach for your foul weather gear. We found ourselves watching the birds more than we did the barometer, and when they turned pink, we turned blue (in spirit, that is).

One item of great importance is a sturdy plastic bucket, not the usual flimsy kind that loses its handle after hard use. As a matter of fact, there should be at least two of these buckets, since they can be lost overboard. They are needed for scooping up sea water for bathing and washing dishes, for catching rain water at the forward end of the boom, for possible fire extinguishing, for use by a victim of seasickness, and for an effective emergency bailer. I have heard it said that there is no bilge pump as efficient as one scared man with a bucket. Fortunately, I've never had to put this theory to the test, but my feeling is that I have the potential for high efficiency.

6

PROVISIONS, STORES, AND STOWAGE

or

Refrigeration Bedamned

Provisioning for an ocean passage that could last for a month or longer will obviously be planned in accordance with whether or not the vessel has refrigeration. We decided against having it, which seemed most astonishing to some people. In fact, a newspaper account of our cruise proclaimed in the very opening sentence: "When the Richard Hendersons left Gibson Island for the Azores on their 37-foot sloop, there was no refrigeration aboard." We felt this denial of a modern convenience was not a reversion to primitivism but merely a sensible simplification of the seagoing way of life that would impose no real hardship. Refrigeration requires the use of generators and/or engines and alternators with accompanying noise, fumes, burning of fuel, and concern about depletion of electricity. Moreover, there is the expense and complication of unnecessary mechanical equipment that can fail and result in food spoilage.

A surprising amount of variety can be had from foods that require no refrigeration. Many fruits and vegetables will keep for a month or more without ice, and, of course, there is a great variety of canned foods available nowadays. In addition, one can carry freeze-dried foods which will keep for ages, but we did not take many of them, because they demand so much fresh water. We did, however, carry dried meats such as salami and chipped beef and a lot of dried fruit.

Sally began buying canned goods for our cruise as early as the fall of 1974. By purchasing well in advance, she could look for specials, and we had the opportunity to sample the food to see if we liked it. Of course, this advanced planning gave her ample time to prepare the cans for stowage. The preparation consisted of peeling off the paper labels (so they could not wash off and possibly foul the bilge pumps) and marking the cans with their contents and dates of purchase. This labeling was done with a nylon-tip waterproof marker made by Dri-Mark Products. All the cans we bought had a shelf life of at least three years, and for the most part we bought cans of heavy metal, so there was no possibility of deterioration by corrosion. We did have a few aluminum beer cans that got damp in a low locker and corroded through after a while. Any thin cans carried in the vicinity of the bilge should have a coat of varnish.

I won't try to list all the cans we took but only some samples of what we liked. They are as follows: Wilson's canned turkey, pork roast, and corned beef; Dak (Danish) bacon and ham; Hormel's knottbuller and beef stroganoff; Underwood deviled ham and roast beef spread; Snow's clams and clam chowder; Gulf Queen shrimp; Swanson's chicken stew and beef stew; Milani Newburg sauce; Red Pack whole tomatoes; Naas Sauce Arturo (for addition to corned beef hash or spaghetti); Del-monte fruit salad, string beans, Italian beans, and asparagus; and Crosse and Blackwell's vichyssoise. Those are specific brands we preferred and that were readily available, but of course there are many other canned foods of which one brand seemed about as good as another. Some of the general foods we liked regardless of the brand were: corned beef hash, franks and beans, meat

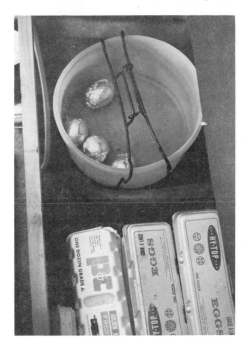

A plastic tub with lemons tightly wrapped in aluminum foil, and the eggs lightly oiled and packed in plastic cartons that were turned over every five days.

balls, Vienna sausages, tuna fish, salmon, lobsters, beef ravioli, Welsh rarebit, chili with beans, beef vegetable soup, chicken noodle soup, cream of celery soup, onion soup, beef bouillon, artichoke hearts, antichoke ensalada, beets, mushrooms, kale, garbanzo beans, olives, palm hearts, petits pois, succotash, Chinese dinners, apple sauce, pears, pineapples, mandarin oranges, and various fruit juices in small cans.

There was an amusing and possibly apocryphal story told about Harry Pidgeon's provisioning. When the famous single-hander was asked what he did for fresh milk, he replied that it presented no problem, for he had been weaned at an early age. His point was well made, that milk certainly isn't essential for adults; however, it is nourishing, and at least one doctor, who is an authority on survival, thinks milk is so important that it should be included in lifeboat emergency rations. We carried it in dried and condensed form but also took whole milk in cans.

Sterilized whole milk without preservatives is canned by Real Fresh Milk Inc. in Visalia, California.

Some of the fresh foods we took that lasted up to three or four weeks without refrigeration were: potatoes, carrots, onions, garlic, apples, Chinese cabbage, lemons, limes, grapefruit, butter, margarine, cheese, and eggs. Other things that last for a week or ten days are: tomatoes, zucchini, cabbage, avocados, radishes, turnips, and bananas. Of course, fruits and vegetables that will ripen after they have been picked should be put aboard when they are green, and they should not be washed, but merely brushed off. They should be stowed in well-ventilated lockers and if possible separately. Don't put apples with carrots or onions with potatoes, as this may hasten spoilage or at least affect the flavor. It's important to inspect the fresh food every day or so, in order to use the items that are beginning to spoil. Also, rot will spread rapidly if spoiled foods are not removed.

We found that Arnold's brick oven bread, double wrapped, would keep for more than three weeks if stored in a dry, well-ventilated locker. The lemons and limes can be preserved by thoroughly drying them, after bringing them to room temperature, and then wrapping them tightly in aluminum foil using a butcher's fold and twisting the ends of the foil. A few lemons came back home fresh after about two and a half months at sea. The eggs were oiled using light vegetable oil (it is not necessary to use Vaseline or grease), and the cartons were turned over every five days to assure that the yolks did not stick to the shells. For long cruises without ice, it is important to buy eggs that have never been refrigerated. We bought ours directly from a farm to assure freshness, and also because we could get them unrefrigerated. None of our 15 dozen spoiled during the passage.

Actually, we did have ice for about the first week of the cruise. Some of our emergency water was frozen in collapsible water bags and kept in the ice box. Unfortunately, as you will learn in Chapter 14, two of three bags leaked after the ice thawed, but the water was not really lost, because it drained into a sealed ice box sump.

All of our dried foods such as flour, pancake mix, corn meal,

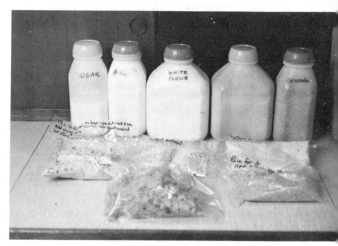

Left: *Canned goods stripped of paper labels, marked with waterproof ink, and stowed by categories in heavy plastic milk bottle crates.* Right: *An assortment of plastic cannisters with screw-on tops and dried goods heat-sealed in plastic bags.*

rice, macaroni, cereals, and dried fruits were heat sealed in small bags of heavy plastic. Sally accomplished this with a special kit called the Dazey Seal-A-Meal, but she preferred using the small Sears boilable cooking pouches called Seal-N-Save. The bags were marked with Dri-Mark for identification and to give the number of servings and the amount of water to be added. For example, a bag might be marked: "Rice, 4 servings, add 2½ cups of water." This system made the preparation simple for anyone who felt like cooking. All the small sealed bags were separated into groups (such as cereals and mixes) and were put into large, heavy, clear plastic bags sold by West Products.

Although we usually ate meals together, anyone could have a snack at any time. We thought this important, because food is a great energy producer and morale booster. One large locker near the companionway was set aside for nothing but snacks. It contained candy bars, crackers, cookies, pretzels, cheese (in a plastic squeeze bottle), raisins, nuts, biscuits, granola, dried salami (Dak's and Slim Jims), and plenty of ginger snaps, which are good for a queasy stomach.

During the fitting-out period, Sally spent a lot of time looking for containers for food and other stores. These containers not only protect the goods and provide easy accessibility, but also they allow more room in the shelves and lockers. She found a great variety of shapes and sizes in cannisters with snap-on tops made by Tupperware. Also, she found some very useful square cannisters made by Family Products, Inc., that had screw-on tops and graduated scales. These were handy for continually used dry goods, such as tea, sugar, salt, flour, raisins, etc. The various containers were of sizes that could be wedged securely into shelves inside the galley lockers.

For her great assortment of spices and seasonings, Sally made a multi-pocketed holder out of waterproof cloth that was hung on the inside of a large locker door. The spices were put in small plastic medicine bottles (obtained from a drug store) which neatly fitted into the cloth pockets. All the bottles and cannisters were marked with Dri-Mark. The galley shelves and locker bottoms were lined with a rubberized cloth called Rubbermaid Shelf Kushion to prevent objects that were not tightly wedged from sliding around. To prevent the movement and capsizing of sauce bottles and the like, I added a fitted wooden rack with round holes for the bottles.

Most of the canned goods were stowed in low lockers to keep the weight low but out of the bilge. We found that large, heavy-duty, plastic milk bottle crates made excellent containers for the cans, preventing them from rolling around and keeping them in groups for easy accessibility. One of these crates, by the way, exactly holds in a tight fit 12 dozen standard egg cartons. Some loose cans were kept in side-opening lockers under the forward bunks, and for these I made plywood pieces that would keep the cans from falling out when the doors were opened. Any loose goods or gear that could roll around or rattle in a seaway were wrapped in sheets of polyurethane foam. For the most part, canned goods were stowed in alphabetical order so they could easily be found in difficult conditions.

Sailing clothes were kept rolled up in lockers or shelves and net hammocks, but for certain soft garments, such as T-shirts

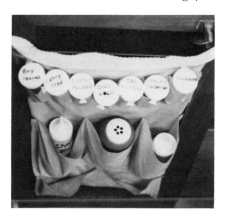

The multi-pocketed holder for spices and seasonings hung on the back of a locker door.

and sweaters, Sally made heavy-duty pillow cases that could be closed with Velcro tape. Thus they could serve both as pillows and clothes bags. Shore clothes to be used after the passage and jackets were kept in the hanging locker. Some of the most fragile clothing such as dresses were hung in plastic waterproof bags, and of course, everything was hung on wood or plastic hangers to avoid possible rust stains. Incidentally, a practical tip for long passages is to steady the hanging clothes with shock cord to prevent chafe.

I mentioned in the last chapter that Sally made a lot of kit bags for stowage. They were cylindrical in shape and made of acrylic cloth of different colors. She would roll a large plate or pot top (depending on the size wanted) across the material to obtain the proper circumference of the bag and use a round piece of cloth slightly larger than the plate or pot top for the bag's bottom. Figure 6-1 shows the various steps in making the bags, which I've dubbed Sal sacks.

It is most important that every vessel going to sea have a recorded stowage plan. Without such a record, items can get lost even on the smallest boat. A few offshore boats have every locker labeled and numbered with the contents recorded in a notebook. We considered doing this but decided that the labels would blemish the handsomely finished mahogany locker doors.

FIGURE 6-1: SAL SACKS

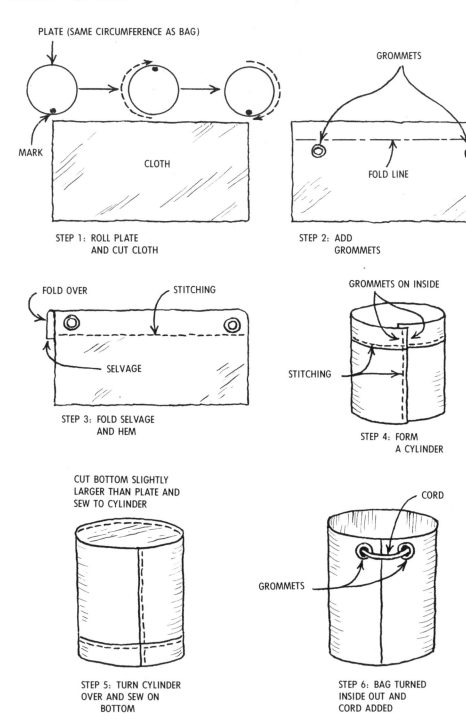

PLATE (SAME CIRCUMFERENCE AS BAG)

MARK

CLOTH

STEP 1: ROLL PLATE
AND CUT CLOTH

GROMMETS

FOLD LINE

STEP 2: ADD
GROMMETS

FOLD OVER   STITCHING

SELVAGE

STEP 3: FOLD SELVAGE
AND HEM

GROMMETS ON INSIDE

STITCHING

STEP 4: FORM
A CYLINDER

CUT BOTTOM SLIGHTLY
LARGER THAN PLATE AND
SEW TO CYLINDER

STEP 5: TURN CYLINDER
OVER AND SEW ON
BOTTOM

CORD

GROMMETS

STEP 6: BAG TURNED
INSIDE OUT AND
CORD ADDED

As an alternative, I drew a diagram of the boat showing every locker and shelf. A system of labels, letters, and numbers on the diagram was identified on a stowage plan list to show the contents of each locker or shelf. This is explained in Figure 6-2 and in the list that follows. In our coding, S stands for starboard and shelf, P for port, L for locker, D for drawer, and B for berth (the sliding pilot berth we converted to a shelf). In addition to the shelves shown in Figure 6-2, there were net hammocks for soft clothes over four of the bunks.

Forepeak—soft drinks; beer; spitfire jib; 13-pound Danforth anchor; light anchor line; life preservers; fresh vegetables (hung in net bags).

Fore bin—35-pound CQR anchor; anchor rode and spare rode; 30-foot anchor chain, 150 feet of spare Dacron line (one-half inch); large tools (saws, surform, brace, rigging cutters, long threaded rod, large wrenches); handybilly; wedges and plugs; spare steering cable and clamps; hoses and clamps; pump for fuel tank; engine lube oil; spare log; extra wire cables (shroud and steering cable); rigging kit; emergency repair kit; beer; soft drinks.

SS1—flammables (solid stove primer, engine-starting booster); CRC lubricant; small Zenith radio; clothes.

SD1—camera and photo equipment.

SL1—canned goods (vegetables).

SL2—(hanging locker) shore clothes, jackets, dry foul weather gear.

SL3—(in floor of hanging locker) largest wrench; wrecking bar; large channel pliers; short pieces of chain.

SS2—(above hanging locker) dark glasses and sunburn cream.

SS3—books; small radio.

SS4—short pieces of line; marlin; shock cord; extra sail stops.

SL4 and 5—clothes; personal items; games.

SL6—snack locker (crackers, cookies, candy bars, etc.).

SL7—safety belts; canned goods.

SL8—alcohol for stove; lamp oil; canned goods.

SB—signal flags; flare kit; drifter; spinnaker.

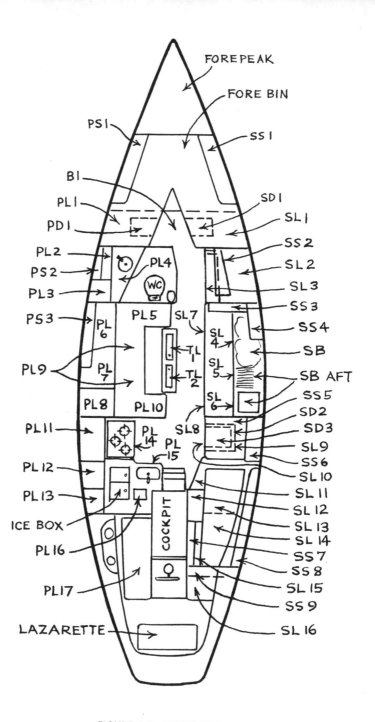

FIGURE 6-2: STOWAGE PLAN

SB aft—navigation books and tables; chronometer; sextant.

SD2—cutlery; eating utensils; galley equipment.

SD3—small readily available tools and small fittings.

SL9—(chart desk) charts; documents; engine manual; etc.

SL10—(under chart table) tool kit; mechanical kit; electrical kit; sail kit; Callbuoy; fire extinguisher.

SS5—hand-bearing compass and Narco beacon (on bulkhead).

SS6—transoceanic radio and RDF (under); flashlight; books.

SL11—(in quarter berth step) ready locker (food for next meal).

SL12—(foul weather locker) wet foul weather gear; shut-off valve for scuppers; life preservers.

SL13 and 14—canned fruit juices and milk; fathometer battery.

SS7 and 8—clothes.

SL15—spare freon and horn; bell; loud hailer.

SS9—blocks; roller reefing and winch handles.

SL16—sheets; guys; lead line; kerosine lights.

Lazarette—shut-off valve for exhaust line; folding deck chair; fenders; dock lines; portable bilge pump; life preservers.

PS1—clothes.

B1—(bilge) speedometer transducer (through-hull fitting).

PL1—canned meats.

PD1—sketching and writing materials; games; flashlight.

PL2, PL3, and PS2—toilet articles; towels; linen.

PL4—shut-off valve for wash basin; first aid kit; paper towels and toilet paper in large plastic bags.

PS3—clothes.

PL5—intake valve for head; egg cartons.

PL6, PL7—clothes.

PL8—dry goods (paper towels, plates, bags, etc.); extra binoculars.

PL9—canned goods in milk crates.

TL1, TL2—(in table) extra compass; gloves; matches; cards; flashlight; etc.

PL10—alcohol tank and shut-off valve; funnels; spare kerosine stove.

PL11, PL12, PL13—dried food; plates; cups; glasses; coffee; tea; chocolate; seasonings; etc. (extra lamp chimney under locker bottom).

PL14—(under stove) liquor.

PL15—bilge pump; scupper shut-off valve; cleaning supplies; spices on door.

Ice box—fresh foods; pots and pans.

PL16—wine; liquors; bottled drinks.

PL17—battery box; buckets; oars; emergency rudder and stock; awning and poles; apples and other fresh vegetables (hung in net bags); storm slides; fuel oil measuring stick.

That is the basic list, although I have not listed every single article carried.

The main considerations in stowing the stores and gear for a long cruise might be summarized as follows: 1) The gear that will be needed most often or quickly in an emergency should be readily available. (2) Heavy gear should be kept low and as much as possible out of the ends of the boat (to maximize stability and minimize pitching). (3) Gear and stores should be stowed so as not to change the boat's trim or give her a list. (4) Canned goods should be stowed low but out of the bilge. (5) Stores and gear should be stowed so that they cannot spill or fall and so that there is a minimum of rattling. (6) Stores and articles urgently or frequently needed should not be kept in a locker under or very close to a sleeping person. Our "ready locker" prevented waking up the off-watch, since the cans needed for the next meal (that were stowed under the bunks) were removed ahead of time and put in the temporary ready location reasonably far from sleepers. Of course, all these stowage considerations cannot always be perfectly satisfied. Some compromises will most likely be necessary. Nevertheless, with careful thought it is not too difficult to figure out the right priorities. When stowing is done with meticulous attention to packing and fitting, it is truly amazing the amount of gear and stores a small boat can carry.

7

THE PASSAGE

or

Some Well-Shaken Wine

There was no chance of our slipping away unnoticed, nor could we leave just when we wanted to, for an official in our yacht club sent out a notice announcing our departure on the afternoon of June 6th. Our friends Nancy and Harry Primrose were also leaving at the same time to cross the Atlantic in their Whitby 42, *Queen Mab,* so a tremendous joint farewell party was scheduled at the Gibson Island boathouse. We appreciated all the attention and well-wishing but would have preferred leaving (with much less fanfare) a day or so later, because *Kelpie* was not quite ready. Sally's school closed that very day, and Sarah had only arrived from college the day before. Furthermore, June 6th was a Friday, and any old salt worth his salt knows that a voyage should not begin on Friday.

The last boatyard job, assembling the jury steering gear, was hurriedly completed on the morning of the 6th, and after that we got underway to take *Kelpie* from the yard to the boathouse, our official point of departure. Buzz White and his gang

Kelpie *about to cast off with a large crowd of well-wishers on the dock and a dramatic sky overhead. (Dr. Roger Batchelor)*

of fine workers gave us a farewell toot with an air horn. I remember wondering whether the horn blast was a salute or a raucous sigh of relief over our finally leaving, for we (along with the Primroses) had been interrupting normal yard work for months, and I had made a special pest of myself by trying to hurry the work and almost hovering over every job that was done.

At the boathouse, *Kelpie* was berthed opposite the mighty *Queen Mab,* where she seemed very small and delicate in comparison. Still, I thought our boat looked cocky and ready for sea, with her new green weather cloths, large radar reflector, jacklines, foredeck nets, and freshly varnished steering vane.

The Primroses, who were taking a year off to circle the Atlantic and cruise the West Indies, were also bound for the

Azores, but by a route entirely different from ours. They planned to go by way of Bermuda, whereas we planned to make one continuous hop from Cape May to the Azores. The reason for our different routes was largely a matter of auxiliary power. A direct course from Bermuda to the Azores runs through part of the mid-Atlantic high pressure zone, where there is a high percentage of calms. That course was fine for the Whitby 42, because, in the words of her designer, Ted Brewer, she "might be classed as an 80/20 (motorsailer)," and she has sufficient tankage for a range of about 1,200 miles under power. On the other hand, *Kelpie* is a pure sailboat with a relatively tiny auxiliary and a mere 20-gallon fuel tank, so I felt, since time was an important factor, it would be better for us to go farther north in order to get well into the westerlies (to say nothing of avoiding the temptation to linger at Bermuda).

We decided on a course along the 40th parallel, because that would be fairly close to the great circle route (the shortest distance) and would get us into southwesterly winds with minimal risk of gales. As it turned out, we were hit with a lot of heavy weather, although the pilot chart for June shows a low percentage of gales south of the 40th. We realized, of course, that no passagemaker can depend on a set pattern of weather; the best one can do is to play the percentages. At any rate, *Kelpie* and *Queen Mab* were to part company just off Gibson Island where the latter would turn south for the Virginia Capes at the entrance of the Chesapeake Bay and then proceed to Bermuda, while we would turn north for Cape May via the C&D (Chesapeake-Delaware) Canal. Hopefully, the two boats would rendezvous at Fayal early in July. Harry had even promised to buy Sarah a drink at the famous Café Sport in the town of Horta.

The early afternoon was spent attending to numerous last-minute details and bringing our personal gear aboard. Before we had finished, friends and wellwishers began arriving, and by mid-afternoon a huge crowd had assembled. Drinks were had, and we received many presents (mostly humorous). The departure of the two boats was quite dramatic, because a squall had been threat-

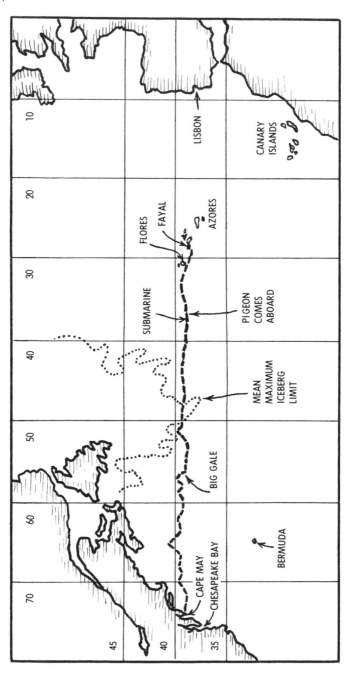

APPROXIMATE TRACK OF KELPIE
ON PASSAGE TO THE AZORES

ening, and just after we cast off, a lovely rainbow suddenly appeared beneath the dark clouds—an omen of good luck. My mother vividly described the scene in a letter: "Horns blew and guns fired and of course I cried. It was so dramatic—the stormy sky and rainbow—all those people and cameras clicking."

We spent that night off Gibson Island in the Magothy River rafted up to *Queen Mab* and another boat belonging to a close friend, and early the next morning we made our actual start. A fresh northwester gave us a thrashing, close reach up the Chesapeake to a quiet cove in the Bohemia River near the entrance of the C&D Canal where we anchored for the night. The following day was spent motoring through the canal and then running with a brisk fair wind down the choppy Delaware Bay. We decided to go through the tiny canal leading from the bay to the harbor at Cape May. It was a relief to get into the smooth waters of the canal, but there was an anxious moment or two passing under a bridge. The tide gauge on the bridge showed a vertical clearance of less than 53 feet, and I figured our masthead to be about 50 feet above the water. Sarah wrote in her diary: "We just made it under the bridge! It was interesting to see the different reactions. Dad (at the helm) kept going— extremely confident; Rip was on the bow just looking; I was in the cockpit praying; and Mom was down below covering her head in her hands." Although I might have seemed confident to Sarah, my heart was in my throat as we went under that bridge. At any rate, our mast was still standing when we later dropped the hook in Cape May harbor.

On June 9th, the wind was not as fresh, but it was still from the northwest, and I was impatient to start offshore. Rip and Sarah made a quick trip ashore to pick up a few more supplies and check the weather at the local Coast Guard station, and then we were ready to get underway. *Kelpie* slowly motored out between the jetties of the Cape May inlet and began to nod her head to the ocean swell. There were not many words exchanged, but we all had strong feelings of excitement mixed with a touch of apprehension. We quietly pondered the great distance to our destination, the uncertainty of the open sea, and the need for complete self-sufficiency for weeks to come.

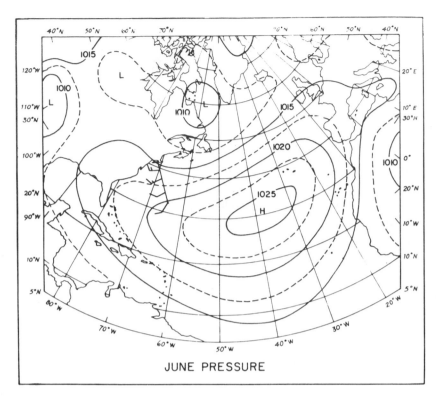

JUNE PRESSURE

The mid-atlantic high with its winds growing progressively light toward the center may shift or extend much farther north. In fact, the Mariner's Weather Log *says that the normal position of the Azores high is centered near 33°N and 38°W in June.*

After hoisting the main and setting the large Genoa jib, we streamed the taffrail log and put the boat on course. Since the coast runs in a northeasterly direction, we decided to head a little south of east in order to get sea room as quickly as possible. Soon the land dropped below the horizon, and it was a bit sobering to think that we would not see solid ground again for the better part of a month. Gradually, the wind lightened, and by dark it dropped out altogether but then suddenly came in strong from the East, forcing us to reef the main and change down to a working jib.

Our first night at sea was a rugged initiation, for it was cold and rough with the head wind gusting up to 25 knots or more.

We had decided to stand lone two-hour watches, because that system gave each person a long period of sleep (six hours), while the time on deck did not seem excessive. We were concerned about Sarah, however, because she had never before sailed at night, and she had very little experience at the helm. Nonetheless, I gave her a close-hauled compass course to steer, and she caught on surprisingly fast. In her own words, "At first I was very scared when Dad gave me the helm—God, I was frustrated, cold, and tired! Dad left me then, and I found I could take my eyes off the compass more and didn't have to turn the wheel so much."

The wind began to die when the sun rose, and by mid-morning we were slatting in a calm. Sails were lowered to reduce chafe, and the engine was run for about an hour, primarily to keep the batteries charged. Despite the electrical drainage, it was important at that point in our passage to keep the running lights on all night and at times to show the spreader lights which illuminate the deck and lower half of the mainsail, because those waters were filled with trawlers that seemed to charge around on highly erratic courses. We had heard that their helmsmen are so busy watching fishfinders, depth sounders, radar, and such instruments that they cannot always look where they are going. This may be an exaggeration, but the safest policy is to assume it is true.

Later that morning, I tried my first offshore noon sight. There is a world of difference between shooting a celestial body on shore (or even from the relatively steady deck of a ship) and taking a sight from a bouncing boat at sea. A technique must be developed, and it takes some practice. Even so, my first attempt gave us a latitude that was not extremely far away from our dead reckoning position, and I was tremendously pleased just to be in the right ball park.

For the next day or so, everything went well. The weather was pleasant, and we were adapting to the new routine. During daylight hours *Kelpie* was rigged for self-steering, but at night I felt that manning the helm would be helpful both to dead reckoning and also looking out. Pelagic life was beginning to

One of the few good sailing days early in the passage. Kelpie's *full-cockpit-width dodger was a great source of comfort when it blew hard from forward of abeam. It is strong and has big enough vinyl windows to afford good visibility.*

appear in the form of porpoises, a few flying fish, and a number of pilot whales. One of the whales came so close that Sally claimed she could smell its breath, which was none too sweet.

The sky that had been so clear began to thicken with clouds on June 12th, and we were in for our first taste of bad weather. The southerly wind kept freshening until we were forced to reef the main and set the small working jib. After awhile, I noticed a small tear beginning to appear at the leech reef cringle, so we handed the main and set the storm trysail. Even with this sail reduction *Kelpie* continued to make six knots on the Kenyon log. About this time, shark fins were seen astern. One of the creatures, dubbed "Mack the Knife," followed us for the next three days.

Friday the Thirteenth lived up to its reputation, for the bad weather continued with periodic rain, gusts piping up to about 40 knots, and a steadily backing wind that eventually put our destination almost dead to windward. *Kelpie* pounded grimly ahead with everyone except myself feeling a bit seasick. We stuck to the starboard tack because that allowed the greatest easting, but we were creeping slightly farther north than we had planned, and it was getting cold—in fact, so cold you could see your breath (that was the June when there was snow in England). The helmsman's standard garb was a sweater, heavy jacket, foul weather gear, waterproof gloves, and a flotation jacket. That night when I went on deck to relieve Sal at the helm, she had the look on her face of a baby girl who has just had her doll snatched away. When I asked her what was wrong, she shouted, "I'm Goddamned scared!" Actually, her words were a bit stronger, but I can't repeat them, because this book is not X-rated. Actually, though, she was a great sport and most uncomplaining considering the conditions.

We came about the next day to head south for what we hoped would be warmer and less boisterous climes. The wind did begin to moderate before long, but the sky remained overcast, and the temperature didn't rise until the morning of the 16th, when the sun finally broke through. What a relief it was to be warm and comfortable again. The seas remained rough for a long while, but for the first time in days, the wind let us up to our proper course.

By June 18th, the wind had completely exhausted itself (as well as us), and we drifted on a glassy swell. This was a most unusual day in that we spoke two ships. The first was an eastbound American freighter, the *Tamara Guilden* from New York,

Speaking the Tamara Guilden. *She has just made a large circle around us and is coming alongside for the second time.*

which altered her course considerably to speak us. She came alongside close aboard and hove to, with most of her crew lining the rail. A voice through a megaphone called down to ask where we came from, where we were headed, and if we wanted anything. Rip expressed our thanks through the loud hailer and asked for a position check. "Just a minute," came the reply. Then to our surprise, the ship got underway, made a huge circle around us and came alongside once again." Thirty-nine north, fifty-two west," said the voice through the megaphone. I was puzzled by this, because I had figured our longitude was close to 62 west, so we asked for a repeat of the position. Again, all of us thought the answer was 52.

After the ship had left, I got to work on my navigation. "Could I be that far off?" I kept asking myself. "Had the ship's navigator known their position when we first asked? Why did they have to circle around us? Could we have misunderstood?" My badly shaken confidence was restored a few hours later, when another eastbound ship changed course to come alongside. She was the German freighter *Anna Wesch,* from Hamburg, and her skipper gave us a position immediately that agreed with ours. It was somewhat disappointing that we had not progressed further, but I was happy to be reassured about my navigation.

At that time, we were not too far from the major shipping lanes leading to and from New York, but it was surprising that two ships would alter course to speak us. I hoped that there would not be too many repeats. As it turned out, there were none, and we did not see another ship, with the exception of a submarine, until we were close to the Azores.

The following day was beautiful. In Rip's words: "Today was our best yet with a sparkling sea, good breeze, clear sky, and nothing to do but lie in the sun and feel good." I told the crew that this was what ocean cruising was really like, but I spoke too soon, for late in the afternoon the sky began to fill with high-altitude clouds and we felt a growing swell that seemed to be coming from a distant storm.

The southwesterly wind freshened until we were forced to shorten sail, and just before dark we could see what appeared to

An overtaking sea prior to the heaviest weather.

be an ugly front to the north northwest. That night we were struck by thunderstorms with alternating lulls and heavy squalls. Confused seas made *Kelpie* roll, pitch, and corkscrew.

We had a rule that the bilge should be pumped periodically, but usually there was no water to be removed. At the end of Sal's watch, however, she was shocked to find that 77 strokes on the pump were necessary to clear the bilge. Needless to say, I too was alarmed, so in the middle of the night we began a frantic search for the leak. I felt sure the source must be a through-hull fitting, but they all looked sound. Sally began to fear the hull had cracked, and she insisted on removing all the canned goods that were stowed under the bunks so we could inspect the hull shell. This was quite a chore at night and in such a seaway, but at least we were able to reassure ourselves that the hull was not damaged. The source of the leak was not discovered, but we found the inflow could be taken care of quite easily with the pumps.

The same kind of weather continued throughout the next day. There were severe squalls with lightning and thunder, rain, and hailstones. In between the squalls we would roll and slat, completely becalmed at times. I got an offshore weather report on WWV, and warning was given for a gale very close to our position. During the night, the wind came in strong from the north, and we lay to, ranging ahead slowly, under the storm trysail. Daylight brought a slight respite, as the wind moderated

An ugly sky and building seas just before it really came on to blow.

a little and the sun tried to break through. We hoisted the small working jib and really started to move. The barometer had begun to rise, and I thought we were through with the worst of the weather, but not so, for at noon the sky to the north grew inky black, and the wind began to blow with a vengeance. I recalled the old adage, "Quick rise after low portends a stronger blow." Rip and I donned our safety harnesses and crawled forward to hand the jib. I kept thinking, "This is not the time to fall overboard."

Even with her jib off, *Kelpie* was making six knots, and that was entirely too fast; so we clawed down the trysail and ran off under bare pole. Our speed dropped to about three knots, but the following seas would push us ahead considerably faster at times. It was my trick at the helm. Sarah was to relieve me at 1400, but it was blowing so hard, I wouldn't let her come on deck. I struggled with the helm for three hours and finally asked for some relief from Rip. By then, the sea was wilder than I had ever imagined it could be. I would hate to estimate the velocity of the gusts or the size of the seas, because I've so often heard blue water men speak with contempt of the "yachtsman's gale" (a ridiculous exaggeration of the weather). All I can say is that it was the worst weather I've ever experienced (and that includes a line squall with winds accurately clocked at more than 70 knots). The scene we viewed was awesome. Seas were huge and confused, with some of the peaks seeming to rear up level with the spreaders. Wave tops were torn off, and the water turned white from the blown spray and streaks of spume. The noise on deck was really deafening. This was the time when Sally was sure we could not survive.

Rip took the helm for about an hour, while I rested below. He was having a hard time holding the stern up, and occasionally a sea would break aboard, half filling the cockpit. I opened the little port in the storm slide to ask Rip how he was doing, and he yelled back, "Dad, I can't hold her much longer!" Once more I crawled back on deck to study the situation. The weather was getting no better, and I felt we had a choice of two tactics: to set the tiny spitfire jib and run off towing drags or else to lie ahull. After some consideration, I said, "Rip, let's try hulling and let *Kelpie* take care of us." So the helm was secured down (with the rudder to windward), and we retired to the cabin. *Kelpie* turned broadside to the wind heeling sharply but not excessively. She did some rolling but skidded off to leeward, dancing away from the seas like a skillful boxer backing off from a flurry of punches.

Down below, it was much more pleasant, although the motion forced us to hang on every minute. Sally took a fall and hurt her back which caused some worry, because she had a lot of pain for a while, but half an hour later she felt all right. The safest place to be was in a narrow bunk behind a tightly strung-up lee cloth. Sally and I got into her extra wide berth together and securely wedged ourselves in to prevent being rolled from side to side. Everyone including myself felt a bit seasick, but our medicines helped a lot. Before coming below, I was actively seasick for the first time since I was nine years old, so that says something about the violence of the motion.

It was much quieter in the cabin than on deck, but still there was a muffled roar from the outside, the banging of halyards on the mast, the clanking of gear in lockers, and the creaking of bulkheads. Every so often there was a loud vibrating smash from a particularly vicious wave pounding the hull, and several times the windows were struck so hard that I looked up to see if they were still intact. Periodically, we would get up to make inspections, pump the bilge, and peer through the windows. *Kelpie* lay ahull for 15 hours and took good care of us the whole time.

Thus we spent the day and night of the 21st. It was Rip's 24th birthday, and Sally had planned an elaborate celebration with a cake and presents, but we could do little more than drink a half-hearted toast with some well-shaken wine.

After the weather cleared on the following morning, we had a glorious day and night of good sailing. But then, damned if it didn't cloud over and pipe up again. Another gale! By this time, we were depressed and exhausted; so the decision was made to once again lie ahull overnight. Thank God the gale was not as bad this time, and we were able to get some needed sleep. This refreshed us somewhat, yet we were still discouraged about our progress. I had hoped the passage could be made in three weeks; however, we had been at sea for two weeks and weren't half way to our destination. I even became a little concerned about depleting our fresh water, and so we strictly rationed ourselves to half a gallon per person per day.

Our bad luck changed after the third gale. The weather cleared, we began to get the expected southwesterly winds, Sally outdid herself in the galley, and our spirits were decidedly lifted. We even found the worrisome leak, which came from the rudder shaft stuffing box (we had been misled into looking for the leak farther forward, because there was a supposedly watertight semibulkhead between the engine compartment and cabin, but it proved to be permeable). I was not able to stop the leak completely, but at least I could tighten the gland and slow the inflow to a rate we could easily live with.

It did turn cold on the 26th of June, but perhaps the chill was partly imagined, because *Kelpie* was then sailing through a finger of the mean maximum iceberg limit as shown on the pilot chart. Those waters did seem a bit eerie, for the sky was misty, and there were strong tide rips with patches of brown gulf weed caught in the swirls. Perhaps those rips were caused by extensions of the Labrador current mixing with the Gulf Stream.

All went well, with good weather and fast daily runs (one being 164 miles), until June 28th when the wind dropped out.

The calm lasted for almost 30 hours, and at the end of that time our spirits were low enough to warrant a pep talk. A rational group discussion cheered us noticeably, and I got Sally to agree that if the calm persisted, we would treat ourselves to some swimming. Up to that point, Sal had been so afraid of sharks that she wouldn't hear of anyone swimming. We had seen sharks, and it is perfectly true that certain kinds can strike very suddenly without warning. Nevertheless, she agreed that our morale needed a boost, and I half convinced her that we could keep an adequate lookout. Fortunately, a breeze soon filled in and we didn't have to risk the sharks. As for cleanliness, we had been able to satisfy this need with bucket baths, salt water soap, Prell shampoo, and Downy, all of which work quite well in salt water (see Chapter 8).

July 2nd was in some respects an unusual day. It was a bit misty with poor visibility, and not too far to leeward Sally spotted a strange object, some kind of structure. Through the binoculars we saw what appeared to be a submarine running slowly on the surface with her conning tower sticking up and her decks almost awash. There seemed to be a number of white cylinders on deck. Could they have been missiles? We could not determine the nationality of the sub (we imagined her to be Russian), and she made no effort to communicate with us. For almost an hour she ran along very slowly on a course that paralleled ours and then suddenly disappeared.

The other unusual event of the day was that we took on a new crew member in the form of a carrier pigeon. It flopped to the deck, where for some time it lay in a state of exhaustion. We fed it cracker crumbs and water, and after a while the bird recovered sufficiently to scramble into a winch base compartment, a literal pigeon hole that was to be its home until we reached Horta. I named the bird Harry in honor of the great singlehander, although Sarah, more steeped in Hollywood than nautical lore, wanted to call him Walter.

By this time, we were getting close to the Azores, and, of course, the sky became overcast so that I could not get any decent sights. Nevertheless, on the morning of July 4th, I was

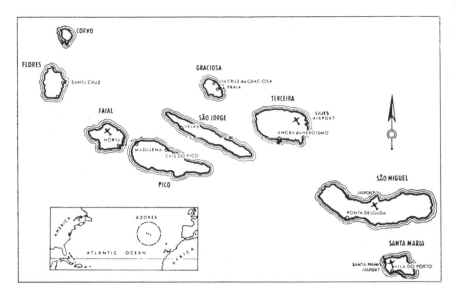

The Azores Islands with small inset showing their location in the Atlantic.

able to catch the sun off guard peeking through the haze and figured that we were only about 50 miles from Flores. A prize was offered to the one who first spotted the island, and at 1300, Rip saw what he thought might be land. He described the event in his diary: "Sitting on the bow I began to notice a dark mound shape that looked like a dark cloud (the sky was full of them) *except* that the edges didn't change. I began to get very excited—summoned everyone to have a look, and Dad said it did look suspicious. Then I noticed ahead an even darker shape, what I had previously thought was a squall, and saw a break in the clouds surrounding it—a mountain's edge! That was it! *Flores dead ahead!* And the small mound-shaped island I'd seen at first was Corvo. As we looked again a cloud cleared over it and the edge came solidly into view. We positively identified it then! We laughed and shouted we were so happy. The amazing thing was that Dad's navigation was right on!" It was amazing indeed, considering my ability as a navigator.

We sailed to within about five miles of Flores. It was a wild-looking island with steep, rugged cliffs and mountains jutting into the clouds. There were patches of green vegetation and occasional villages nestled among the rocks. "Just like the island in *King Kong!*" exclaimed Sarah and Rip. We had all grown fond of Harry the pigeon, but he was leaving numerous droppings around the boat, and he'd become so tame that he began flying into the cabin, once alighting on my head while I was asleep. So we decided Harry must go. We threw him into the air, thinking he would fly to Flores, but no indeed. He circled around and came back to the boat. He knew a good deal when he had it.

The sail between Flores and Fayal was beautiful—a clear night sky filled with stars and a fresh northerly wind that, in my imagination at least, seemed to be an extension of the famous Portuguese trades. On my morning watch after the sun came up, I saw two enormous sperm whales dead ahead. They were nearly twice as long as *Kelpie* and seemed to be sleeping or perhaps basking in the sun. I had to alter course sharply to avoid hitting them. It was a little frightening to think of colliding with such formidable creatures in the dark. I wondered whether they would have been there at night and whether they would have been able to sense our presence at the last moment before collision. One night early in the passage, we passed by a large ghostly shape that was illuminated by phosphorescence, and we thought it might have been a whale. But whatever it was, I would not like to have run it down. The incident served to reinforce my belief that some risk is involved in going to sea on a boat that is very lightly built.

The island of Pico is well known as being an easy landfall because of its pyramid-like mountain, which rises up to 7,613 feet above sea level. However, the navigator can be misled by atmospheric conditions. On that morning of July 5th, the air seemed completely clear, and yet there was a slight mist or haze that prevented us from seeing Pico until we were about 35 miles away. Rip was the first to spot it—a giant pyramid with a lower mass of land at its foot, which was the island of Fayal. As we drew closer, we could see that Fayal was in the foreground. It was fascinating to see our destination gradually take on sharper definition and color as the hours passed.

We were bound for Horta, said to be one of only two decent

harbors in the Azores (the other being Ponta Delgada at San Miguel). Horta is on the east side of Fayal, and we elected to sail around the south side of the island and then northward up the channel between Pico and Fayal. That course was somewhat shorter and would avoid a lee shore. I had read that the channel can be difficult when sailing northward in a fresh northerly partly because of the venturi effect of the wind blowing through the gap, but *Kelpie* is a good performer to windward, and we had only a short beat to Horta.

Late in the afternoon, we reached Capellinhos, the western-most point on Fayal, and this was really something to see, because an undersea volcano had erupted in 1957 creating a new peninsula of lava, rock, and ash. The recently formed crater was so new that it had little vegetation, and in the setting sun its reddish hue contrasted markedly with the greens and grays of the island. Passing close to the southern shore of Fayal, we were charmed by the quaint villages, churches, and cultivated fields that made a patchwork pattern on the mountain slopes. I experienced the strangest kind of sensation when looking at the shore,

Closing on the island of Fayal. On the left the Isle Nuova created by the Capellinhos volcano in 1957 and 1958.

a kind of dizziness or slight lack of balance; my stability could only be restored by glancing in the opposite direction, at the open sea. Probably my balancing mechanism had become so accustomed to the motion of the sea that I became disoriented when confronted with something that didn't move.

Kelpie rounded a small crater off Castello Branco Point in the last rosy glow of twilight amid a swarm of birds that had been disturbed from their nesting holes in the rocks. We would have to enter Horta after dark or else lie to offshore until daylight. Normally, the latter course of action is the safest in strange waters or uncertain conditions, but entering Horta during fair weather at night did not seem difficult and we decided to do so.

The short passage up Fayal Channel went well except that we had to keep a sharp lookout for small, open, fishing boats that were not well lighted. At about 2200, we rounded the large beacon at the end of the long breakwater that forms the east side of Horta's harbor. We motored into the crowded little anchorage almost blinded by bright flood lights on the breakwater and nearly ran into a large mooring buoy. After circling around a few times, we finally found a spot to drop the hook. Ordinarily, yachts make fast to a long quay at the southern end of the breakwater, but we decided to anchor because our yellow quarantine flag was flying, and we had not officially entered or been granted pratique (permission to land). However, I was a little nervous about anchoring, because I had read that the holding ground is poor, and there are numerous chains on the bottom that can be fouled.

Once the hook was down and the boat was tidied up a bit, we gave *Kelpie* a congratulatory pat and drank a toast to our arrival. Then, as we were sitting in the cockpit admiring the scenery, we heard a female voice from across the harbor yelling, *"Kelpie, Kelpie!"* It was Nancy Primrose aboard *Queen Mab*, which had arrived the day before. We launched the dinghy and rowed over for a jubilant reunion, a proper gam, and the best ice-cold beer I've ever tasted.

The next morning we were boarded by the port inspector, who gave us some forms to fill out and showed us where to

Quayside at Horta with Jud on the afterdeck. The weather cloths are a bit forlorn after the beating they took during the bad gale.

moor alongside the quay. The anchor came up without much fuss, although there was a piece of old rotten line caught in the flukes. We made fast to a bollard and large iron ring in the rough quay wall near *Queen Mab.* All our fenders were needed, for there was a surge that made *Kelpie* bump and grind like a burlesque queen.

A fascinating aspect of the breakwater is that along the entire length of its 10-foot-high wall, for more than a quarter of a mile, there are inscriptions of visiting yachts—their names, visiting dates, and sometimes even a sketch of the boat or perhaps an insignia or burgee painted in bright colors. These graffiti are actually encouraged by the inhabitants of Horta, which exemplifies the hospitality and friendliness shown to visiting sailors. Of course we also had to leave our mark, so eventually we found a blank spot on the wall next to the inscription of the well-known American yacht *Ondine,* and Rip, standing

Our mark on the wall along with the inscriptions of some famous yachts. We didn't learn until sometime later that it is considered bad luck not to leave your mark.

atop an oil drum, painted in bold letters, *"Kelpie–Queen Mab,"* with our hailing port, date, and the Gibson Island burgee. When we were at Horta, by the way, the harbor was full of interesting offshore yachts. Most came from England or Europe, but some came from as far away as New Zealand. For a brief while, the famous cruising couple Mary and Humphrey Barton, in their sturdy sloop, *Rose Rambler,* were made fast just astern of us.

Saying farewell to Rose Rambler. *Her skipper, Humphrey Barton, is a well-known small-boat voyager, author, and founder of the Ocean Cruising Club.*

Horta is a picturesque town with an easy-going, old-world atmosphere. It has all the modern conveniences that are really needed but has not been spoiled by an "OD" of progress. The white and pastel-colored buildings with red tile roofs make a tessellated pattern against the background of lush, green hills that surround the harbor. The main sidewalks are broad, clean, and decorated with mosaic tiles. There are two splendid hotels, and our first thought after coming ashore was to get a room with a private bath and to spend about an hour apiece in a hot shower washing away the Atlantic brine.

We chose the Estalagem de Santa Cruz, an unusual government-run hotel built inside an old fort located on the edge of the harbor. Our double bedroom was luxurious, with heavy antique furniture and a private balcony from which we had a clear view of *Kelpie* alongside the quay. Our plan was to use the room and boat alternately, with Sally and I staying in the hotel one night while Rip and Sarah stayed on *Kelpie,* and vice versa the next night, with Sally and I afloat and our children ashore. The arrangement worked out very well, for the boat was watched and protected, yet everyone had a chance to luxuriate ashore. We usually got together for dinner at the hotel, where delicious full-course meals were served. Breakfast there was especially delightful to my way of thinking, because we could eat on our balcony in the sun and watch all the activity in the harbor. Incidentally, prices at the hotel were most reasonable.

One of the first things we did after arriving at Horta was to look up Peter Azevedo, proprietor of the tiny Café Sport. Peter is known to most transatlantic sailors as being a real friend of the small-boat voyager. But he is not just friendly, he holds mail, gives sound advice, and takes a personal interest in the welfare of visiting sailors, no matter what their nationality (he speaks five different languages). Peter and his recently deceased father had for decades been compiling records of boats that stopped at Horta. We were treated to a look at some of the many scrapbooks containing information, messages, photographs, and sometimes sketches of the visiting boats.

One of the ways that Peter was helpful to us was in finding a

The famous Café Sport managed by Peter Azevedo, friend of the blue-water sailor and a port officer of the Ocean Cruising Club.

good home for Harry the pigeon. The bird would not leave *Kelpie* even after we moored alongside the quay. But Peter knew a man who raised carrier pigeons and was willing to take Harry off our hands. The man paid us a visit on the quay, and I could see at once that he knew how to handle birds. He did not speak our language, so we tried to communicate in French, but ended up by using gestures and pidgin English (pun intended). At any rate, we all felt sure that Harry would be well cared for.

We spent a week on Fayal and enjoyed every minute of it. A taxi cab tour around the island was arranged by Peter, and we were treated to such sights as mile after mile of lavender hydrangea hedgerows, Flemish windmills, vineyards and terraced fields under tidy cultivation, numerous churches built of lava rock, cliff-side views of the sea, and a spectacular look into the Caldiera, the island's largest crater. Some of our time was spent at the local yacht club, where we met and talked to many of the visiting yachtsmen. We even paid a visit to the whaling factory, just a short walk from Horta, which dramatically came to life when a large sperm whale was killed and towed ashore.

Sarah with the harbor at Horta in the background. This port is a favorite stopover for transatlantic sailors.

Rip and I watched the interesting but gruesome sight of the whale being cut up and processed. As I will mention later, we are very much against the slaughter of whales, but at least the Azoreans kill very few, partly because whaling is still done in the old-fashioned way, with hand-held harpoons from open boats.

On July 10th, Ed Karkow and his crew arrived to spend a few days on Fayal before sailing *Kelpie* home. You may recall from Chapter 1 that Ed was to sail *Kelpie* back to Gibson Island, thereby giving the Henderson family a chance to visit Europe while the boat was being taken home before the beginning of the peak of the hurricane season. We telephoned Ed immediately after our arrival in Horta, and we all agreed that it was too late in the season for us to continue on to Lisbon if we wanted to have *Kelpie* sailed home that year. The risk of hurricanes is too great after the early part of August.

Ed's crew consisted of his 13-year-old son, Jon; Neal King, a middle-aged decathlon champion from Chicago; and Neal's 17-year-old son, Steve. A couple of days were spent in getting *Kelpie* ready for her return trip, repairing gear and stocking up, and by July 12th she was ready to leave. The old girl didn't have much of a rest from her ocean sailing, but after bumping against the quay wall and having her decks covered with lava dust carried by a southerly wind from Monte da Guia crater, I think she was looking forward to going back to sea. Sally and I had the strangest feeling watching *Kelpie* leave. It just did not seem right that we were not on board.

On the return trip, *Kelpie* made a slow passage to Bermuda.

A typical street scene in Horta. For the most part we found the town charming, picturesque, and refreshingly free of tourists.

Ed's theory was to sail far south to get into the trade winds, and he sailed down to about 26° 30′ N. latitude, but the steady trades were not there. A direct course might have been a good deal quicker, but Ed says that if he should do it again, he would sail almost southeast from the Azores to reach the trades sooner and perhaps go farther south during the middle part of the passage. The choice is between sailing a relatively short course in an area having a high percentage of calms and head winds or sailing a much longer course (perhaps half again as far) in an area that has a high percentage of fresh, favorable winds.

Kelpie's return passage, although slow, went well except for a fair amount of seasickness, and when she reached Bermuda, Ed's wife and daughter joined him for the final leg home. Neal King had to leave for Chicago, but Steve, who was developing into a splendid sailor, stayed aboard. *Kelpie* pulled into Gibson Island on August 20th, little the worse for wear after her two and a half months of ocean sailing, except that her dark green topsides were faded and caked with salt, she wore a belt of gooseneck barnacles around her boot top, and her stanchions were bent inboard somewhat from the battering of our gale. Ed and his crew had brought her back in good shape as expected. I was very touched by a remark made by Steve King before he stepped ashore. After more than a month on *Kelpie*, when many teenagers would be scurrying ashore like rats from a sinking ship, Steve said, "You know, Mr. Henderson, I can hardly bear to leave this boat," and I had the distinct feeling that he really meant it.

8

ROUTINE AT SEA
or
Larks and Owls

Although the word "routine" often suggests monotony, life on a
small boat at sea is surprisingly varied. I think the weather is
primarily responsible for this, because it controls or affects
many activities, such as changing sails, taking sights, bathing,
sitting in the sun or huddling under the dodger, pursuing various
chores and interests, manning the helm or relaxing while self-
steering takes charge, and so forth. Of course, there are other
activities that must be quite regular regardless of the weather.
The chronometer must be wound at the same time every day,
the eggs should be turned, the bilges must be checked periodically, the rigging should be examined every day, the log is read
and recorded with regularity, fresh foods must be inspected
every day or so, etc. Perhaps the most regular aspect of the
routine at sea is standing watches.

Our system for watches at night was one person at a time on
deck standing a two-hour trick at the helm. I felt the system
was a good one, because it meant that when you came off

watch, you could look forward to six consecutive hours of sleep (provided, of course, the off watch was not called for a sail change or an emergency). Our daylight watches were a little more flexible, but we figured on each person getting at least two hours of sleep during the day for a total of eight hours of sleep in a 24-hour period. A chart of our watch routine is shown in Figure 8-1. The square symbols represent meals (usually they were square meals), while the wheels represent time at the helm, and the triangles with arcs (symbolizing sextants) represent the times spent navigating, or at least taking sights when the weather permitted. The dark portions of the chart are the hours of sleep. Notice that each person had the same hours each night for steering and sleeping.

The watch schedule was organized as shown on the chart so that I would be on deck at dusk and dawn for star sights and at noon for sun sights and so that Sally would be awake during meal times and available to help me during noon sights. Also, an attempt was made to arrange the watches according to whether a person is a "lark" or an "owl." This is Sally's classification of a person's sleeping habits. An owl likes to go to bed late and arise late, while a lark likes to turn in early and arise early. Rip and Sarah are both owls, so they came off watch late at night; while Sally is a lark, and so she turned in for her six hours of sleep early in the evening. I don't quite fit into either classification, because I like to turn in fairly early but get up late (perhaps there should be a sloth category). Another consideration was that we felt it would be desirable for Sarah's watch to follow mine, because she was the least experienced, and I could be sure she was in full control before I left her. Sometimes I would linger awhile and we would have some of our best talks. Of course, those were rare occasions when I would be allowed to do most of the talking due to Sarah's condition of not yet being fully awake.

The night watches were sometimes beautiful and stimulating, especially during clear weather when the sky was full of stars. But when it was cold and stormy, no one, including myself, looked forward to a lonely two hours at the helm. Still, there

FIGURE 8-1: WATCH ROUTINE

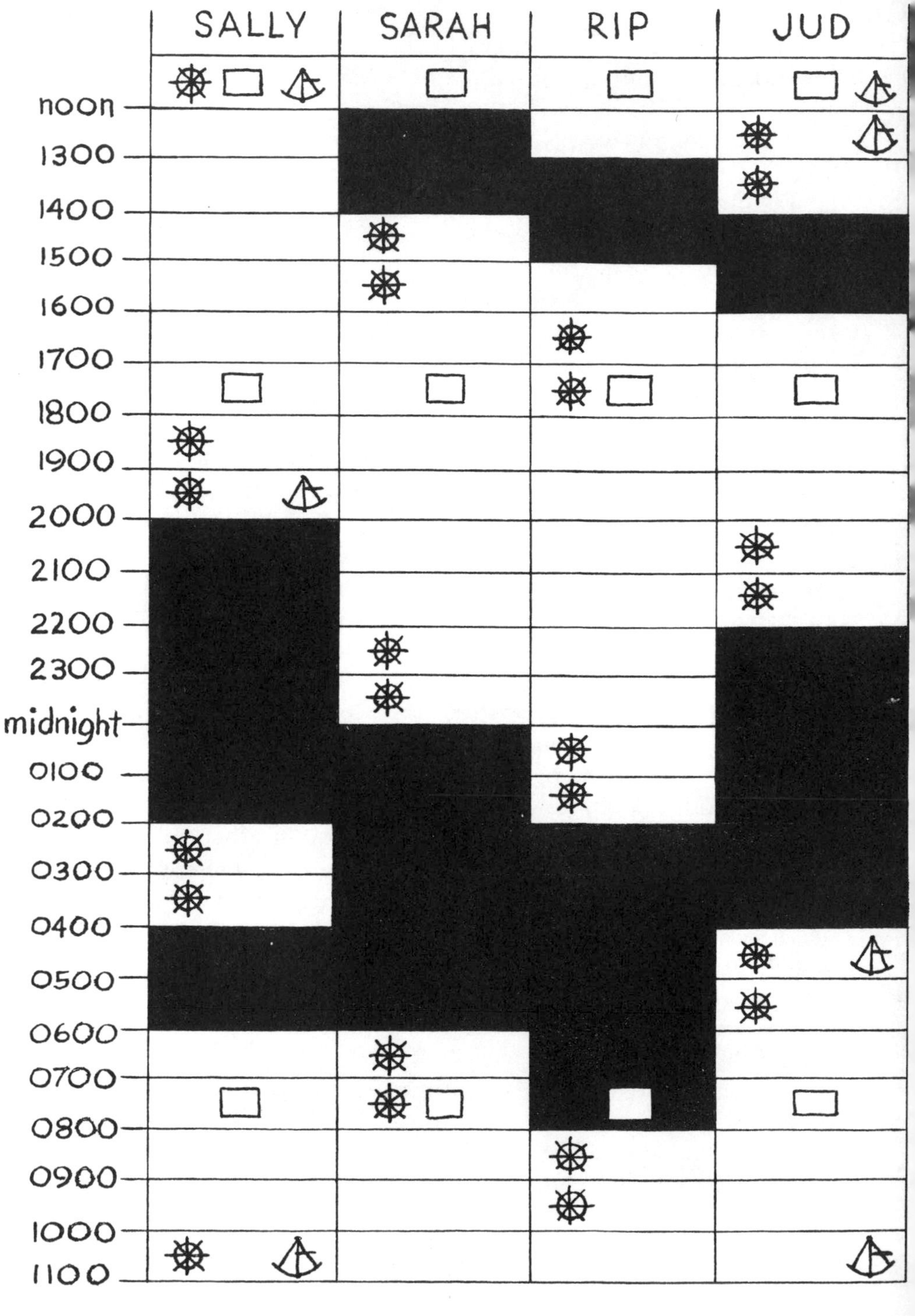

was pleasure to be had from looking forward to your hours off watch, and the bad weather made you appreciate to the fullest extent the bliss of a warm, dry bunk. The unpleasant times on deck were made much more bearable by being properly garbed and having a hot drink readily available. Every night Sally made a thermos full of hot coffee, bouillon, or Ellis energizer (see Chapter 11), which was placed within easy reach of the helm.

Our standard night watch garb has already been described, and I mentioned that we carried a whistle and small strobe flasher in the pocket of the helmsman's flotation jacket. One night when Sarah was on watch, I heard her call out in a startled voice. I scrambled out of the quarter berth to see a strange red light being reflected below from the cockpit. Sarah was being illuminated by a ghostly glow that went on and off at regular intervals. She had a surprised expression on her face and was looking around for a ship with a search light. It turned out that the strobe flasher in her pocket had inadvertently been turned on, and the powerful light was shining through the orange jacket, causing her to glow like a lightning bug.

We had some strict safety rules for sailing at night. The person on watch was always secured with a safety line, and he or she could never leave the cockpit unless there was another person on deck. There was a rule that the sea had to be scanned for ships every ten minutes. This meant that the watch keeper had to turn entirely around and make a 360-degree visual sweep of the horizon.

On one occasion, during my watch, when we were nearing the Azores, I failed to make a full-circle sweep, and we could have been run down. It had been raining, and I had the hood of my foul weather jacket pulled up, which limited my peripheral vision. I turned completely around and thought I had covered the entire horizon, but not so. Several minutes later, I heard what sounded like breaking surf. Turning my head, I saw the bow of a large passenger ship bearing down on us perhaps 300 yards away. This was the first ship, not counting the submarine, we had seen in 14 days, and we were not in a steamer lane. I changed course immediately and turned on the spreader lights.

The incident could not really be considered a close call, but it was a little too close for comfort. The lesson I learned, of course, is that a lookout has to be sure he scans a full 360 degrees. This may not be as easy as it sounds, because at sea there are no land marks that can be used as reference points. One has to use a part of the boat or perhaps a star at night for a reference to be sure there is no sector of omission.

In one area of our sea routine some sailors might consider us a bit reckless. We seldom used running lights when far offshore and away from steamer lanes. The reason for this was to conserve the batteries. I felt it was more important to have the batteries when we really needed them than to take a chance on depleting them when there was little risk of meeting a ship. Of course, being unlighted means that strict watches must be maintained, and a continual lookout is necessary, but in my opinion, that is the best form of protection. Typical sailboat lights are quite often nearly invisible, and lookouts on ships in mid-ocean are often lax, especially nowadays in the era of radar and small crews. Incidentally, we had two lead/acid, 12-volt, 100-ampere batteries, one being charged with the engine's generator and the other with an alternator. We ran the engine every few days for an hour or so to keep the batteries up. There was a standing order that I was to be called (if I was below) whenever a vessel or lights were seen.

A definite routine was followed when going off watch. The helmsman being relieved would be sure his replacement was fully awake and was steering the proper course. Then, the taffrail log would be read and the mileage and course sailed would be entered in the log book along with any pertinent remarks about the weather. Next, the bilge would be pumped and the number of strokes required to clear it would be entered in the log. A bilge record was important for us not only because of the stuffing box leak described in the last chapter, but also because *Kelpie* (like most modern boats) has a fairly shallow sump in her keel, and if it should fill, the bilge water would roll up into the lockers under the bunks. Before turning in, the off-going helmsman would shed his foul weather gear and stow it in or just outside the foul weather locker alongside the companionway to be sure that no salt water got into the main cabin.

It is well known that anything that becomes wet with salt water will remain damp, even on a clear day if there is a lot of humidity in the air. That is why we made a special effort to keep wet clothing out of the main saloon. I made the mistake early in the passage of going forward to secure a sail without first putting on my boots, and I regretted doing so, because my deck shoes (Topsiders) got wet, and they remained damp for many days. Most of the time, by the way, we wore light-weight rubber boots called Totes, and we found them very satisfactory. They are easy to put on and take off, can be folded compactly, and have skid-proof soles.

Of course, our dirty clothes had to be washed in sea water, but Sally found that a fabric softener removed most of the salt from the clothes and allowed them to dry. We used a half cup of Downy softener to a bucket of water. For washing ourselves, our hair, and the dishes, we found that Prell shampoo worked very well. Occasionally, salt water soap was used, but it was much less satisfactory. We did allow ourselves the luxury of washing our faces and brushing our teeth with fresh water. For

Rip taking fiendish delight in dumping a bucket of water on Sarah's head during a hair wash.

this, a plastic squeeze bottle was kept in the locker behind the head sink so that we could keep track of just how much water was used. An interesting fact is that we found our hair needed washing less frequently at sea than at home. Probably this was because the air is so much cleaner at sea.

On most points of sailing *Kelpie* can be rigged quite easily for self-steering, but the helm was manned most of the time for several reasons. First of all, the lookout is usually more reliable when he is at the helm, because he is forced to be alert. It is all too easy to take a snooze under the dodger when the boat is steering herself. Second, dead reckoning is more accurate when there is a helmsman steering, because he is looking at the compass and can average out the course and keep track of the headings when the boat is yawing. Finally, when there is a crew of four, it is not a great hardship to take turns steering by hand, and it gives each person a responsible job and reduces the risk of boredom.

The wheel rigged for self-steering. The lines leading off the top of the drum attach either to the jib sheet and shock cord or else to the vane gear's steering lines. The white knob on the wheel drum is a clutch that can be pulled out to disengage the self-steering arrangement for adjustment purposes or emergency manual steering.

Nevertheless, we did rig for self-steering every so often during the daylight hours. Usually we did this when there was more than one person on deck to improve the lookout and to assure that if a person should happen to fall overboard there would be someone on deck to turn the boat around for a pickup. Our QME self-steering vane gear was described in Chapter 5 and illustrated in Figure 5-1. A photograph shows how it was rigged on *Kelpie*. Notice that steering lines are led from a drum on the steering wheel through blocks attached to the cockpit coaming and then back to the vane's drum. When the gear is set in operation, the vane is weathercocked into the wind, and the steering lines are attached to the vane with snap hooks. If the boat strays off course, the wind strikes the vane on its side (rather than edge), causing it to tip over on its horizontal axis, thereby exerting a force on the appropriate steering line which, of course, turns the helm and brings the boat back on course. Lead counterbalance weights make the vane return to an upright position when its edge once again faces the wind. We found that it was necessary to use a rubber strap (supplied by the manufacturer) or a piece of shock cord to limit the degree of the vane's tipping. The QME works best, of course, when the sails are adjusted for perfect balance (so that there is no weather or lee helm). One day we had the boat so perfectly balanced under the QME that when I disconnected the steering lines, *Kelpie* kept on steering herself for over an hour. Apparently, she didn't realize that she was not being controlled by the vane.

Actually, we only used the vane gear when the wind was forward of the beam. When the apparent wind came from abaft the beam, we found it simpler and more effective to tie the jib sheet to the wheel drum's leeward steering line. The steering line that leads off the top of the drum on the opposite (windward) side was attached to a length of elastic shock cord that was made fast to the windward coaming. With this arrangement, if the boat begins to head up, the jib pulls harder and turns the wheel to leeward so that the boat bears off to her proper course. But if she should bear off below the proper course, the jib pulls less hard and the shock cord makes the helm correction. The method usually worked very well when broad or quarter reaching. On a run with following seas, however, neither system of self-steering was satisfactory. Twin headsails would have been our best bet with the wind aft, and that is what we would have had for the kind of trade wind passage that produces fresh following winds for day after day. If there had been just one less crew member, I would have seriously considered a more elaborate vane gear with underwater parts, probably an Aries gear, produced by the same company that made our wheel steering drum.

For entertainment when off watch, we did a lot of reading, although I did somewhat less than the others because of my navigation duties. Sarah seemed to be the most ambitious intellectually, as she tackled some heavy Russian history. I took along a number of sea stories, including some books from the "Mariners Library" (published by Adlard Coles in England), a splendid collection of small-sized hardbacks that fit neatly into our small bookshelf. I was delighted to have Rip read, for the first time, Erskine Childers' fictional cruising classic, *The Riddle of the Sands*. Our good friend Arthur Sherwood gave us *The Wilderness World of John Muir* with the inscription, "May you draw from the sea as Muir drew from the mountains." We all enjoyed that book and were inspired to a fuller appreciation of nature no matter what the setting.

Sarah, who was in charge of entertainment, brought instructions for macramé and a number of games, such as playing cards, backgammon, crossword puzzles, and Scrabble. There are some games that have magnets on the movable pieces, and these are practical on a boat, but I was opposed to having them aboard because of the possibility of compass deviation. Sarah especially liked to listen to the radio when the reception was good, and that gave us all a contact with the real world; but she had a limitation, mostly self-imposed, on rock and roll. After all, *Kelpie* gave us plenty of that.

Of course, navigation, sail handling, and cooking were very much a part of the daily routine, but they should be discussed in some detail; thus each of these activities gets a chapter of its own.

9

NAVIGATION

or

"When You Get the Chance, Grab It"

Before our cruise, I knew very little about celestial navigation, and I'm far from an expert now. However, I learned enough to get us there. It might be said that I am a navigator in the same sense that a flyer who can walk away from a landing is an aviator. Nevertheless, my technique gradually improved throughout the cruise, and we did make our landfall "right on," as Rip expressed it.

There are a lot of navigation courses available for the aspiring offshore sailor, and many of them are excellent, I understand, but most require a prerequisite course in basic piloting. Since I didn't want to waste valuable time going through the basics (though it would have done me no harm), I didn't enroll in a standard course. Fortunately, our harbor master at Gibson Island, Captain George E. White, who formerly was a merchant ship skipper and navigation instructor, was more than willing to give Sally and me (along with some other yachting folk) a number of lessons, free of charge. Sally decided to join me in the study of celestial navigation, because she has always had an interest in the stars, and she wanted to help me and be able to take over in the event that I should become incapacitated. Of course, I was delighted to have her join me not only for back-up reasons, but also because we could help each other learn and share the experience. As it turned out, Sally did no actual navigating on the cruise, but she helped me with the observations by being the time keeper and was able to find a few errors in my calculations when my figuring of our position made no sense. Also, I became confident that she had learned enough to take over in an emergency.

We learned the H.O. 214 method that works from a convenient assumed position and has a different book of tables for each 10 degrees of latitude (published by the U.S. Naval Oceanographic Office). In addition, we used Volume I of H.O. 249 (published by the Defense Mapping Agency Hydrographic Center) for selected star sights. Although we often shot the stars and planets, we mainly relied on observations of the sun. My drill was to take a morning sun sight at around 1100 or earlier (local time), then a noon sight, and another shot of the sun around 1300. The line of position (line on which we were located) obtained from the 1100 sight would be advanced along our course the distance we traveled between the morning and afternoon observations, and it would cross the 1300 line of position to give us a running fix. The noon sight would give us an accurate latitude, another line of position, and a rough longitude check.

Theoretically, a sight at the time of meridian passage (when the sun is exactly on your meridian, at noon) will give your longitude accurately, provided you know the exact time at Greenwich, England, because the sun's Greenwich hour angle (GHA), which can be thought of as corresponding to the sun's longitude, is listed in the *Nautical Almanac*. Thus the sun's GHA should equal your longitude at the precise moment of meridian passage. In actual practice, however, there are difficulties with this simple method, because one cannot always be sure of exact noon. Obviously, it will come when the sun is at its highest point in the sky (after rising and before descending), but the top of the curved path is quite flat, and the sun seems to hang at the highest point for a few minutes. Thus it is extremely difficult to know the precise moment of noon, especially so when the navigator is making his observation from the bounding deck of a small boat. For best results it may be preferable to take a sight well before noon and another after noon when the sun has the same altitude, and then average the times to find out the time of meridian passage.

Latitude from the noon sight is normally quite accurate, because no time is really needed. In our case, with the summer sun being north of the equator and ourselves being still farther north, it was only necessary to determine how far the sun was north of the equator and how far we were north of the sun, and the two measurements were added to give our latitude. The sun's distance (in degrees) from the equator, called its declination, is found in the *Nautical Almanac*. The boat's distance from the sun, called the zenith distance (the zenith being a point directly over the observer's head), is obtained by taking a sight with the sextant (which gives the angle between the sun and horizon) and subtracting this angle from 90 degrees. For example, on June 25th the sun's altitude at noon was 73 degrees, 24 minutes. Subtracting this from 90 degrees gave a zenith distance of 16 degrees, 36 minutes, and adding this figure to the declination of 23 degrees, 23.8 minutes north gave a latitude of 39 degrees, 59.8 minutes north.

A simplified description of the procedure for the morning and afternoon sights using H.O. 214 is as follows: First an observation is taken with the sextant to obtain the sun's altitude; and, at the same instant, time is noted from the chronometer, which is always kept on Greenwich mean time (GMT). Then certain chronometer and sextant corrections are made, and the *Nautical Almanac* (or the *Air Almanac*) is entered to find the GHA and declination of the sun at the time (in Greenwich, England) the sight was taken. This might be considered the sun's longitude and latitude if it were projected directly down to earth. Next, we assume our boat's position, based on dead reckoning (DR),

Jud taking a sun sight. Notice the lanyard around the neck as a safeguard against dropping the sextant.

i.e., keeping track of compass courses steered over distances recorded by the taffrail log. The GHA is subtracted from the assumed longitude (or vice versa) to obtain the local hour angle (LHA), which is the angular distance between the sun and us. The assumed longitude is merely the position near our DR position that makes the LHA come out in even degrees to simplify arithmetic.

Now we are ready to enter H.O. 214 with our assumed latitude and local hour angle, which is listed in the tables under HA. Opposite the hour angle, under the proper declination (obtained from the *Almanac*), the altitude and azimuth (bearing) of the sun is given. This listed altitude is known as the computed altitude, and we compare it with the observed altitude (our sextant shot with corrections applied). The difference gives what is called an altitude intercept, the distance our actual position is away from or toward the assumed position. After this, our assumed position is marked on a plotting sheet, and we draw the azimuth line in the direction of the sun. The intercept distance is marked toward or away from the sun along the azimuth, and a line of position (LOP) is drawn at right angles to the azimuth. If the computed altitude is greater than the observed altitude, the true LOP (the line you are actually on) is farther away from the sun (and vice versa if the observed is greater than the computed). The standard memory aid is Coast Guard Academy (CGA) or Computed Greater Away. As said before, at least two LOP's are needed to obtain a fix.

That is the basic procedure in a nutshell. The method might be thought of as finding the sun's altitude through tables after considering the vessel's location to be at an assumed position, and then comparing this angle with the actual measured altitude to find out the variance and thus the true line of position. One point that could lead to confusion is the local hour angle. In H.O. 214 the LHA can be considered east or west, but in the newer tables, such as H.O. 229 or H.O. 249, the LHA is measured in a westerly direction through 360 degrees. For the details of entering the tables and for general theory, a navigation course is advisable, but there are several good books on the subject that can be a real help. The one Sally and I like the best is *Celestial Navigation Step by Step* by Warren Norville, and I'm not saying so because it is put out by the publisher of this book. Norville deals with H.O. 214 (as well as 229 and 249), and his book is comprehensible yet adequately thorough for the yachtsman.

I must admit I often had trouble with star sights, although not with planets. The H.O. 249 tables simplify finding the stars and reducing the sights, but the problem for me had to do with the technique of making accurate observations. Stars have to be shot at dusk or dawn, and there is a very limited time when they are distinct and there is also a clear horizon. I often found that when I could clearly see a star, the sky was too dark to see the horizon, or vice versa, when the horizon was distinct there was too much daylight to see some of the weaker magnitude stars. I did find out that dawn sights are much easier, but I seldom took them because of my reluctance to wake up one of the crew to relieve me at the helm, although I could have rigged for self-steering on some occasions.

A possible problem is being sure you have the right star. H.O. 214 is a great help in this respect, because it lists various ideal stars in groups of seven, and the tables give their computed altitude and azimuth. A listed star is most easily located by precomputing from the tables its height and bearing. Then the navigator sets his sextant to the proper angle, aims it in the right direction, and he should pick up the right star. We also had a Rude star finder (No. 2102-D), which consists of an opaque plastic base and transparent templates showing star locations at various latitudes, but this device is really not needed if you have the H.O. 249 Volume I tables. With the star finder or H.O. 249, you need your assumed latitude and the local hour angle of Aries (a reference point on the celestial equator). The GHA of Aries is found in the *Almanac* and your assumed longitude is applied to find the LHA of Aries.

Polaris (the north star) is particularly handy for a latitude check, even though it is rather dim, because it is so easy to identify, and its altitude is very nearly equal to your latitude. Of course Polaris is not exactly over the north pole; so a number of corrections must be applied for any accuracy.

Occasionally, I took sights on Venus and Jupiter (or Mars). These planets were easier than the stars for me, because they are so bright and steady (non-twinkling). Their identity can be determined from the *Almanac* or with the Rude star finder.

Our sextant is a full-size model made by International Nautical in Japan to specifications of Weems and Plath. Although I've read at least one disparaging comment about Japanese sextants, we had no problems with ours. It is a good quality instrument for a moderate cost, slightly over $300. The sextant weighs three pounds and has a 7 X 35 monocular, a micrometer drum with a vernier marked with a two-tenths-of-a-minute scale, and a light on the arc and micrometer drum. A feature I like very much is the variable density polarized shades, which allows any shading variation with one simple adjustment.

We also carried for an emergency back-up a British-made, light-weight, plastic Ebbco sextant. This is a remarkable instrument for its price, about $50, and it has many features of the large, expensive sextants. However, I might be concerned about the shades for prolonged use. Some authorities say that certain cheap shades may not block out all the damaging sun rays that are not always in the visible spectrum. I have two friends who sustained some permanent damage to their eyes from improper shading, and an eye doctor friend told me that the shades on some of the cheaper World War II sextants could have microscopic cracks that might admit harmful rays. It would certainly be advisable to have such shades checked by an optician.

Undoubtedly, the greatest difficulty for the novice navigator has to do with sextant technique. This cannot be learned from books but must be developed through practice at sea. Of course, the basic technique can be learned ashore where there is an unobstructed horizon (or by using an artificial horizon), but practice is really needed from a moving deck. Every navigator seems to have his own style of balancing himself and holding the sextant steady. Many people lean against the mast or rigging when taking a sight, and some seem to have developed a special knack of gripping the shrouds with their shoulder blades. The easiest method for me was to sit on the cabin top with my back braced against the turned-over dinghy.

Needless to say, the sight should be taken while the boat is on the crest of a wave so that the true horizon can be seen. The sextant must be exactly vertical, so it should be rocked slightly from side to side like a pendulum in order that the celestial body makes an arc as it swings above the horizon. You can be sure the instrument is vertical when the bottom of the arc just touches the horizon. At that instant the time is noted.

We used a fairly standard method of noting time. While I took the sight, Sally, or occasionally Rip, stood by with the time piece, pencil, and notebook. After bringing the sun or other celestial body down close to the horizon I would say, "Stand-by," and then, "Mark!" when the body kissed the horizon. Sally or Rip would note and record the time at that instant and then write down the sextant angle after I had read it off the arc's index, micrometer drum, and vernier scales. If there is no assistant, the navigator can use a stopwatch, which he starts when the horizon is kissed. Then he can later read the chronometer time and subtract from it the minutes and seconds shown on the stopwatch to obtain the GMT of the sight.

Sometimes it is difficult for the beginner to locate the celestial body in the mirror of his sextant. A fairly simple method is to set the index arm at zero degrees on the arc's index scale and aim the sextant directly at the celestial body so that the reflected image and direct view of the body can both be seen together through the sighting scope. Then the sextant is slowly lowered while the index arm is slowly pushed away from you so that the reflected image stays in view until the body is brought down to the horizon. A word of warning, however, is to be sure the shades for direct viewing are used if you are taking a sight of the sun. An alternate and more commonly used method is to precompute or simply estimate the celestial body's altitude and preset the arm on the index scale. Then the sighting scope is aimed at the horizon directly under the object, and if the image does not appear in the mirror, the arm is moved back and forth until the image does appear. Still another method is to turn the sextant upside down, aim at the body, and bring the horizon up to it; but I'll have to admit, this system seemed awkward to me.

For our time piece, we carried a World War II Hamilton chronometer watch that is spring-driven and hung on gimbals. But what we actually used was a battery-powered Timex Quartz wrist watch that was much handier and more accurate than the chronometer. The Timex lost only one and a half seconds during our 27-day passage, and that is remarkable when you consider it only cost about $50.

Of course, we were able to check the time with our radio. For this, we had an 11-band Zenith Transoceanic (costing about $300) that also could be used as a radio direction finder by mounting the set on a swivel base. We seldom had any trouble picking up time ticks or offshore weather (broadcast at eight minutes after the hour) over station WWV, Colorado, on frequencies of 2.5, 5, 10, or 15 MHz. In addition, we took a cheap time-check radio crystal-tuned to 5, 10, and 15 MHz. It is called a Timekube and was sold by Radio Shack for about $30 when we bought it. I understand this particular radio has been discontinued, but I've heard that Radio Shack now sells a more expensive model called the Astronaut-6. We found the Timekube was very satisfactory when not too far offshore, but reception became poor when we were less than half way across.

The chronometer and sextant boxes were fit snugly into a large, specially-made, open box that was screwed to the after end of the starboard pilot berth just forward of the chart table. As said previously, this sliding berth was only used for stowage. With its mattress removed, it made an ideal shelf for large items that needed easy availability. Just forward of the sextant and chronometer, we secured a heavy plastic milk bottle crate that tightly held the large-size navigation books, such as the H.O. 214 and 249 tables. Navigation equipment must be immediately available, especially the sextant and time piece, because the opportunity to take a sight may only be momentary on an overcast day. Sally and I never forgot the words of Captain

The sextant and chronometer in their readily available location.

White when he advised taking every possible sight in cloudy weather. He said, "When you get the chance, grab it."

Aside from the H.O. tables, Warren Norville's book, and the *Nautical Almanac* already mentioned, other navigation-related books and publications we carried were as follows: The *Air Almanac; Reed's Nautical Almanac; American Practical Navigator* by Nathaniel Bowditch; *Dutton's Navigation and Piloting* by G. D. Dunlap and H. H. Shufeldt; *Celestial Navigation for Yachtsmen* by Mary Blewitt; *Primer of Navigation* by G. W. Mixter; *How to Navigate Today* by M. R. Hart; *Self-Taught Navigation* by R. Y. Kittredge; *Book of the Sextant* by G. D. Dunlap and H. H. Shufeldt; *Noon Sight Navigation* by A. A. Birney; *Electronic Navigation Made Easy* by J. D. Lenk; *Radio Navigation Aids* H.O. 117A (Atlantic and Mediterranean area), published by the Defense Mapping Agency Hydrographic Center (DMAHC); *Lists of Lights and Fog Signals* Publication 113, published by the DMAHC; *U.S. Coast Pilot 3,* published by

Just forward of the sextant box is the plastic milk crate that neatly holds the large navigation tables, Pilot books, and Sailing Directions that are clipped into the white loose-leaf notebooks.

the National Ocean Survey; *West Coasts of Spain and Portugal Pilot,* British Admiralty publication No. 67 (obtained from Captain O. M. Watts, Ltd., 49 Albemarle Street, Piccadilly, London); *Sailing Directions for the West Coasts of Spain, Portugal and Northwest Africa and Off-Lying Islands,* H.O. 51, published by the U.S. Naval Oceanographic Office; *Worldwide Marine Weather Broadcasts,* published by the U.S. Department of Commerce; and *Tidal Tables for Europe and West Coast of Africa,* published by the U.S. Department of Commerce.

More information concerning the above government publications can be found in Bowditch (*American Practical Navigator*). That book, by the way, comes close to being indispensable for ocean cruising. It is published by the U.S. Navy Hydrographic Office and is known as H.O. Publication No. 9. Most of the aforementioned, privately printed books may be obtained from International Marine Publishing Company, the publisher of this book, or perhaps the Dolphin Book Club.

Among the charts we took were: *Standard Time Zone Chart of the World,* H.O. 5192 (N.O. 76); *Great Circle Sailing Chart of the North Atlantic Ocean,* H.O. 1280 (our straight-line course drawn on this chart gave us the shortest course); *North Atlantic Ocean—Northern Sheet,* N.O. 121, Mercator projection (for plotting our track); *Position Plotting Sheets,* N.O. 973 (for plotting our daily positions); *Pilot Chart of the North Atlantic Ocean,* N.O. 16 for June, July, and August; and of course numerous charts for the Azores and the coast of Portugal (in the event we had had time to continue on to Lisbon). The Department of Commerce puts out a booklet called *Authorized Nautical Chart Agents* that lists the various sellers of National Ocean Survey charts and publications.

In the voyage planning stage especially, Pilot Charts are extremely valuable, for they show the percentage of calms, gales, wind direction and strength, current direction and velocity, fog, ice limits, etc., as well as steamer lanes, ocean station vessels, magnetic variation, mean atmospheric pressure, and so on. Maurice Bailey told me that he prefers British Routing Charts to American Pilot Charts because the former give more information

The chart desk with hand bearing compass mounted so that it can double as a telltale. The magnifying prism shows the compass heading, which can be read quite easily from a prone position in the quarterberth. The wristwatch on the desk is the Timex quartz that was checked for accuracy with the Timekube (directly under the books) or the Zenith Transoceanic radio (next to the books).

about the wind. The U.S. charts give the average force on the Beaufort scale, while the British equivalents give a percentage of Beaufort frequencies, Forces 2-3, 4, 5-6, and 7-12. However, the *Oceanographic Atlas* Publication No. 700, published by the U.S. Naval Oceanographic Office, gives essentially the same wind information is the routing charts. A legend explaining the system is shown in Figure 9-1 (see page 125).

Another publication that may be of some use is the *World Port Index,* Publication 150, published by the U.S. Naval Oceanographic Office. It gives the location of major harbors, the *Sailing Direction* in which they are found, the harbor chart on which they are shown, size and type of harbor, shelter afforded, depths, tide, pilot and quarantine requirements, supplies, repair facilities, and so forth. A considerable amount of useful information on ports and harbors can be obtained from the Cruising Information Center at the Peabody Museum in Salem, Massa-

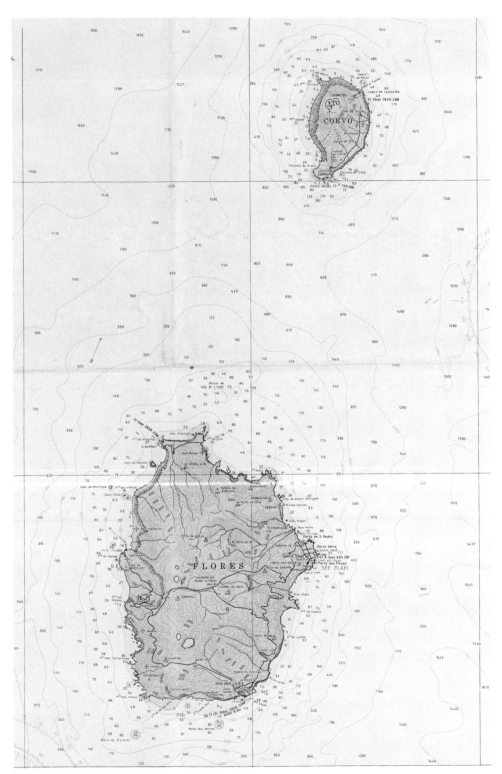

Our first landfall, Flores and Corvo, the westernmost islands of the Azores group.

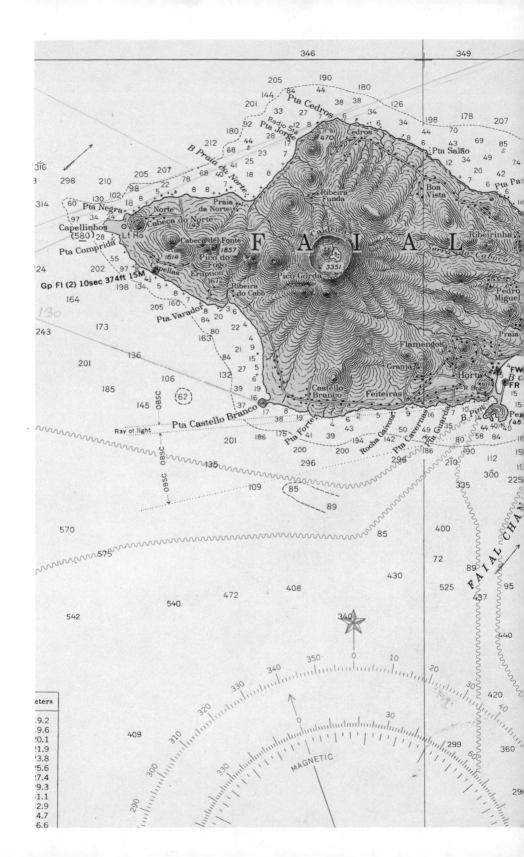

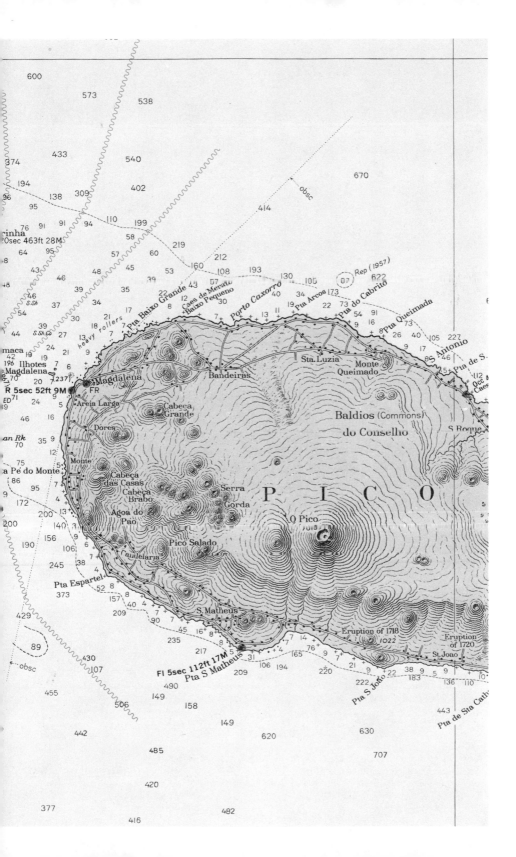

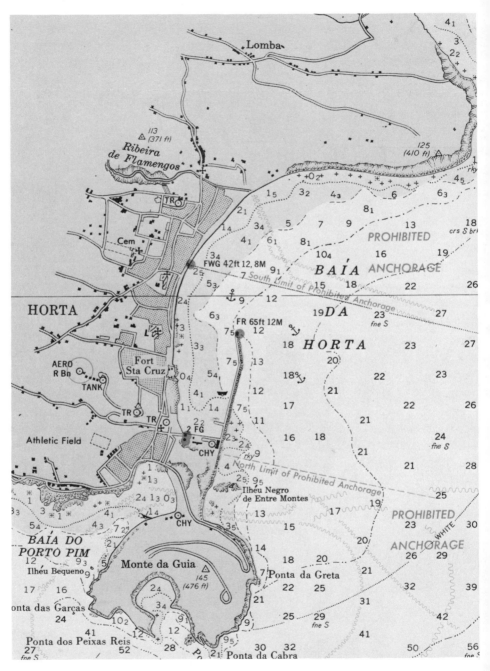

Horta with its long seawall that makes a good artificial harbor. Boats may be sprinkled with lava dust from Monte da Guia on a strong southerly wind. The chimney (CHY) on the north side of Monte da Guia is the whaling factory. There is a broad sand swimming beach just north of the factory.

FIGURE 9-1: OCEANOGRAPHIC ATLAS WIND ROSE

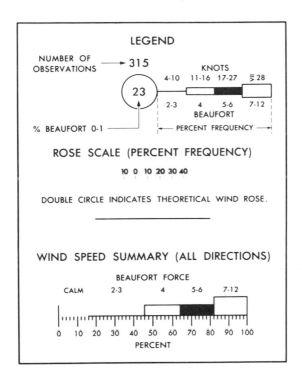

chusetts. Although this is a Cruising Club of America organization, I believe it will assist any inquiring yachtsman. Of course, there are a number of useful cruising guides that cover foreign waters, such as *The Cruising Association Handbook* for the British Isles and parts of Europe.

Our dead reckoning and piloting equipment included a small Negus taffrail log, a spare Walker log (borrowed from a friend), and a Weems and Plath hand bearing compass. The latter doubled as a spare steering and telltale compass. It was carried in a specially made holder mounted above the chart table, and from my quarter berth I could see the boat's heading on the instrument's magnifying prism. The distance-recording Negus log

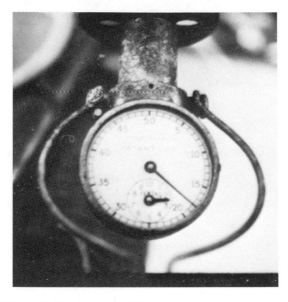

The little Negus taffrail log that is compact and accurate but that froze up on the way home.

is a fine little device that is no longer made, I understand. It did freeze up on the return passage, however, and I suspected the cause to be lack of lubrication; but when I took it apart, I found a couple of ball bearings missing. How they disappeared is a mystery to me. The bronze rotator that was towed astern was hauled aboard every few days and painted black with a nylon-tip waterproof marker (Dri-Mark) so that it would not attract fish. Of course, one has to be alert that the rotator does not foul with weed.

In the early part of the cruise, I was somewhat concerned that our dead reckoning frequently did not agree with our position figured from celestial observations by as much as 20 miles. At first I thought my celestial navigation was off, but later I decided that the DR was inaccurate. This is understandable, because courses are not always steady, and we were often in unknown currents where there are apt to be some eddies or meanderings. Furthermore, I suspect we had some slight compass deviation. Our steering compass, a Danforth Express, was very accurate before the cruise. In fact, Buzz White had remarked that its deviation card looked like his grade school report card, almost all zeros. Our loading for the cruise probably affected the compass, however, and we didn't have time to swing ship properly before leaving. Not that this was a serious problem, because all we really needed was a DR close enough for running fixes and proper assumed positions. Eventually, I learned to check the compass by sun azimuths, and this was a help, but the deviation was really not significant.

For radio direction finding, we had the Zenith Transoceanic mentioned earlier as a back-up set, but our primary RDF was a Gladding Corporation Gulfstream made by Pearce-Simpson. We bought it at a discount, for about $150, from Goldberg's in New York. The set has a lot of desirable features, such as pre-tuned VHF weather (for coastal sailing), a visual null meter, and a sense antenna (for reciprocal ambiguity). We did have a recurring problem, however. The rotating direction-finding antenna was loose and wobbly, so that the electrical connection would frequently break, causing a spasmodic reception. We reported the problem to Goldberg's and they took back the set and sent it to Pearce-Simpson for repair. We got the same set back again, repaired, but only temporarily. Despite the fact that we handled it with the utmost care, the set developed the same problem again after we put to sea.

Before making our landfall on the island of Flores, we were able to pick up the radio beacon there. However, it was quite indistinct and we needed to use the RDF's beat frequency oscillator to bring it in. Although H.O. 117A showed the beacon to have a range of 100 miles, we could actually pick it up from farther away, but curiously enough, we could not hear it from a considerably closer distance. I wonder if this could have been from coastal refraction due to the rugged terrain. Soon after sighting Flores, we were able to pick up a strong signal FIL (in Morse code) that was not listed in H.O. 117A. We later found out that it was the airport (on the coast) at Fayal, and for the life of me I can't understand why it was not included in 117A. That publication is supposed to include all aeronautical beacons useful to the mariner, and we had the very latest edition. There is a Horta beacon (HOR) listed, but that signal was much weaker.

Of course, our visual landfall was a thrill, especially for me, having the navigation responsibilities. I think Richard C. McCurdy described the feeling perfectly in an article called "Navigation: For the Yachtsman" that he did for *Yachting* magazine (August, 1969). He wrote, "It is one thing to go along on a trip and look over the shoulder of some navigator while he makes a landfall. It is quite another to make a landfall yourself. Then you join the fraternity, and acquire a certain regard for others who have experienced this extraordinary feeling. There is, of course, the sense of responsibility. There is the sinking feeling when the data contradict, and the extra caution until things straighten out. There is the horrid period when you should have made land and you haven't, and the equally horrid moment when somebody unexpectedly sees something. But then there is that glorious thing that happens when, miraculously, the So-and-So Islands *are* there, *really* there. You have never believed it like you do then."

It was very comforting and reassuring for me to know that Sally could navigate. She didn't do it, but she was helpful, and I felt she was capable of taking over my job. In fact, I would have been happy had she done so. In this, I apparently don't share the feelings of Eric Hiscock. When Sally asked the famous circumnavigator if his wife Susan helped him with his navigation, he drew himself up indignantly and replied (with tongue in cheek), "Would I prod her cakes?"

10

SAILS AND SAIL HANDLING

or

It's Breezing Up

For this cruise, *Kelpie* carried nine sails: mainsail, storm trysail, 150 % No. 1 Genoa jib, No. 2 cruising Genoa, lapper, No. 2 working jib, spitfire jib, drifter-reacher, and spinnaker. The latter sail was only taken in case Ed Karkow wanted to use it on the way home or in the event we really needed the extra speed it could give under the right conditions. I have never felt the modern parachute spinnaker, with its great belly and being attached by three corners only, is a seamanlike sail for offshore work, especially when sailing shorthanded (Francis Chichester called it a "lubberly sail"). The No. 2 working jib, storm trysail, and drifter-reacher were made for us by Murphy and Nye of Annapolis, and the spitfire, a Hard product, was a leftover from our previous boat. All the rest of our sails were Hoods that came with the O-38, and they were a delight to handle, because they were made of soft cloth that contained no resin filler.

Sail stowage was no problem, because the mainsail was always on the boom, of course, and the trysail was permanently bent on under the main, while two jibs were usually carried hanked to the headstay. The remaining two heavy jibs were lashed on the spare bunk in the forward cabin, while the drifter-reacher and spinnaker fit snugly in the sliding pilot berth that had been converted to a shelf, and the spitfire was stowed in the fore-peak. The reason for carrying two jibs hanked on was that it facilitated changing. Normally, a jib of the next smaller size would be bagged or stopped to the rail under the jib that was set. Then, if the wind increased, the hoisted sail could be lowered and unhanked as it came down, and the smaller sail could be hoisted immediately.

Figure 10-1 shows the relative sizes of the headsails, and it can be seen that we were fairly well covered for every strength of wind. About the only jib we didn't take on the cruise was a large, light-air, No. 1 Genoa with maximum overlap, but that sail is rarely needed on an ocean cruise, because it is intended for racing to windward, and its foot cannot be properly raised for good visibility and to avoid scooping up seas. All of our jibs, with the exception of the drifter-reacher, had luff lengths a bit shorter than the headstay so that short tack pendants could be added. A pendant not only raised the foot for visibility and wave clearance, but it also prevented the foot from chafing on the bow pulpit and life lines. The small jibs also had head pendants of appropriate lengths in order to keep the wire portion of the wire-rope halyard on the winch. Otherwise, the splice joining the wire and rope parts of the halyard possibly could have been pulled apart.

The drifter-reacher is made of two-ounce Dacron, and it has an overlap of 162%, which means that its LP (a perpendicular from luff to clew) is 162% of the base of the fore triangle (the distance from the stem head to the fore side of the mast). This is an excellent sail for light-air reaching because of its size and light weight and also because it is cut with a high clew. The latter feature prevents excessive twist, that is, having the area aloft fall off and luff, when the sheet is eased. Also, of course,

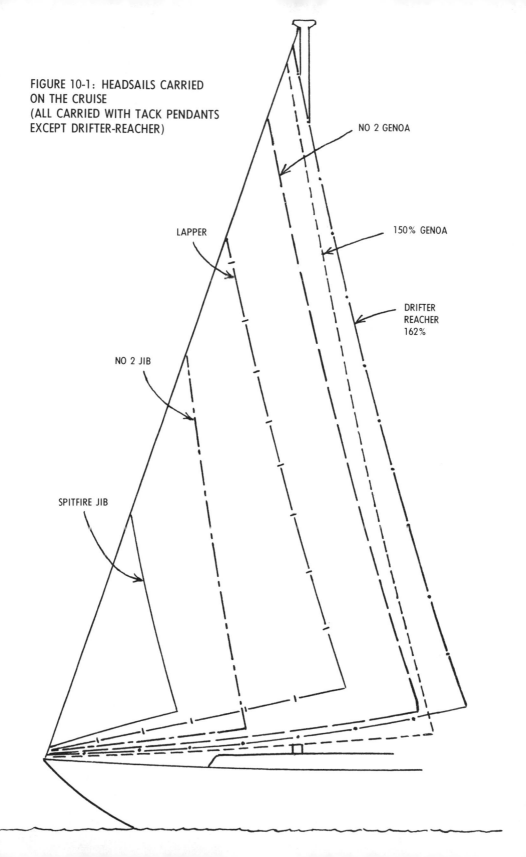

FIGURE 10-1: HEADSAILS CARRIED
ON THE CRUISE
(ALL CARRIED WITH TACK PENDANTS
EXCEPT DRIFTER-REACHER)

NO 2 GENOA

150% GENOA

DRIFTER
REACHER
162%

LAPPER

NO 2 JIB

SPITFIRE JIB

the high clew affords good visibility. The sail is usually set flying on its own luff wire, but there is one hank at the head and one about halfway from head to foot to prevent excessive sag, when close-hauled. When I say close-hauled, I don't mean strapped in tight. The sail should never be carried hard on the wind. In my opinion, a light-weight reacher is a vital sail for any ocean cruiser, especially one with limited engine power.

Our 150 % Genoa, of course, was intended for fresher winds and for windward work. It is miter cut, has a stretchy luff, and is made of 6.5-ounce cloth. It can be seen in Figure 10-1 that the No. 2 Genoa is slightly smaller and has a higher clew. It has a wire luff, and I expected it to be the workhorse, but we actually used the 150 more often, because it is a faster sail. When *Kelpie* was overburdened with the larger Genoa, we usually preferred to change down to the lapper jib. This is a slightly overlapping eight-ounce working jib with a fairly high clew, and it is important for medium-heavy-weather work.

For very strong sailing winds, perhaps over 30 knots, the No. 2 working jib was used. As can be seen in Figure 10-1, this sail is considerably smaller than the lapper, and its LP is less than three-quarters of the base of the fore triangle. The jib is heavily constructed of eight-ounce Dacron, triple stitched, and it is small enough to be used as a storm jib. In other words, it can be used with the storm trysail for heaving to, that is, stopping headway by backing the jib to counteract the forward drive of the trysail while the helm is secured down.

The spitfire jib is a tiny "pocket handkerchief" with an area of only 42 square feet. When I was trying it out one day before our cruise, a friend on a nearby boat remarked, "I'd hate to be aboard when you have to use that." As it turned out, we never had to use the sail. I considered setting it to run off in the big gale but decided to lie ahull instead (our storm tactics will be discussed in Chapter 12). The spitfire was designed to double as a riding sail to be set on the backstay, and it had a wire leech and removable full-length batten to inhibit flapping. We occasionally used it on our previous boat for riding purposes, to stop excessive yawing when lying at anchor.

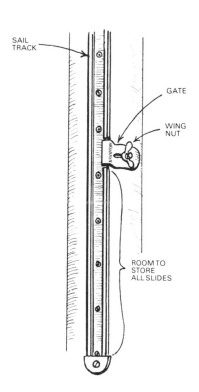

FIGURE 10-2: MAINSAIL TRACK WITH GATE

SAIL
TRACK

GATE

WING
NUT

ROOM TO
STORE
ALL SLIDES

Carrying the storm trysail and no. 2 jib.
The trysail sheet is led through a block
on the winch base. If the trysail were
hoisted higher, its clew could be se-
cured to the main boom, which might
be a better arrangement when constant
tacking is necessary.

For the storm trysail, I considered adding an extra track to
the mast, so that the sail could be hoisted easily immediately
after the main was lowered. I eventually decided that another
track would not be necessary, however, since the one for the
mainsail was fitted with gates. The system for changing from
mainsail to trysail was not difficult, because the trysail was
permanently bent on under a gate. Before the main was lowered
the gate was opened, and as the sail descended, its slides were
run off the track through the gate (see Figure 10-2). Then the
luff of the main was wound around the boom and stopped, and
after the halyard was transferred to the trysail, the smaller sail
was ready to hoist. Of course, this method necessitates putting
the mainsail's slides back on the track when the main is hoisted
again. This is not a great problem, however, because the gates
permit putting on the slides working from tack to head rather

than from head to tack, which is a much more difficult and tiring procedure due to the fact that the top part of the sail must be held up while bending on. Furthermore, bending a sail is normally much easier after a blow has abated rather than while the weather is deteriorating.

When shortening down in a blow, we found it easier to set the trysail than to reef the main deeply. Also, I felt we had a stronger rig with the trysail, which was especially made for heavy weather, and it was always carried sheeted to the side deck so that there was no danger of the boom flailing about and causing an injury. Of course, we did have a means of reefing the main, with roller reefing or a jiffy system, and a shallow reef was no real problem; but I felt that the trysail was superior in many ways to the deeply reefed main in a real blow.

A few miscellaneous thoughts on offshore cruising sails are as follows: Sails should be triple-stitched or at least double-stitched. There should be ample patches wherever chafe can occur, and on certain heavy-weather sails consider a double-rolled tabling (folding over the edge twice) for extra strength. This should be discussed with the sailmaker, as it could cause some wrinkling. Heavy weather sails should have extra strong leech and foot lines, because the free edges of a sail can wear quickly from constant flutter in a long spell of heavy weather. Tightening the leech (and foot) lines will alleviate the flutter, but the lines are seldom strong enough. Some offshore sailors have recommended a hollow leech with no battens on the main-sail, but I disagree. Battens allow more sail area, prevent leech flutter and curling, and in general better control the leech. They don't cause much chafe if they are properly made and have proper pockets. Battens should be smooth with rounded corners, should be shorter than their pockets, and should be securely tied in (don't rely on offset pockets to hold the battens in). High-clewed jibs not only allow greater visibility and avoid scooping waves, but also they alleviate excessive twist when reaching. Heavy weather jibs need not be made of extremely heavy cloth, because of their small size. Luff yarns and telltales are just as important on a cruising boat as on a racer, since they facilitate proper trim. Soft, unfilled sail cloth has greater initial stretch than has resin-filled cloth, but it generally has longer life and is much easier to handle on an offshore cruising boat. Jiffy reefing is fine at sea, but the cringles must be extra strong and there should be a means of lacing up the bunt. Sometimes the loose bunt can fill with water even when laced up, so consider putting a drain hole or two in the sail.

Rip and I were the sail handlers, and we usually worked as a team, although we sometimes went forward alone if conditions were not too bad. When we worked together, of course, sail changing was much easier, but it often meant that one of us would have to be called from a sound sleep. On one occasion Rip entered in his log, "Awakened early by Dad's voice: 'Rip, it's blowing up! We've got to get the trysail on!' It's funny but every time I hear that expression 'blowing up,' I think of the world literally exploding—and I start to laugh. Isn't it strange that I continue to laugh at something so stupid? I must be cracking up." Stupid or not, it helps to have a sense of humor when you have to crawl out of a warm bunk to struggle with a flailing sail on a pitching deck in the dark.

Our night-time procedure was to turn on the spreader lights, don safety harnesses (and life jackets if the weather warranted wearing them), and snap on to the windward jackline. This was a line (described in Chapter 4) on each side of the boat that allowed uninterrupted travel of the safety lines' snap hook from the cockpit to the mast. Once at the mast we could resnap on to any convenient part of the rigging to enable working with both hands. Early in the cruise, we had a jackline running from the mast to the foredeck, but it was soon abandoned, because it got in the way.

I had expected that changing headsails on the foredeck would be the most difficult operation, but it turned out to be surprisingly easy in all but the most extreme conditions *if* the person at the helm bore off and ran downwind while the change was being made. Many sailors, including myself, are so used to changing headsails while thrashing to windward during a race, heeled down and with the spray flying, that they don't realize how easy the operation is when running off. With the wind aft there is less of it, there is less water on the deck and less motion, and most important, the headsails are blanketed.

Our greatest difficulty changing sails seemed to come from the main halyard fouling the spreaders. *Kelpie* has short spreaders, and many times we changed from mainsail to trysail or vice versa while close reaching in a seaway. When there was a lot of slack in the halyard, it would often whip around to leeward of a spreader and foul. I never found a completely satisfactory solution to the problem, but obviously slack had to be kept out of the halyard, and usually this was accomplished by one person pulling down on the halyard while the other person manned the winch. We had to be extremely careful when performing the operation alone. For an offshore cruising boat that never races, it might be wise to have fairly long spreaders, not only to alleviate halyard fouling, but also to decrease loading on the shrouds. Short spreaders require greater shroud tension.

The main halyard winch is a reel type that can be dangerous if it is not handled with care. However, our Barient winch is safer than some, because it has a screw-toggle brake that allows gradual easing, and the mainsail can be hoisted with the brake on so that if the handle should slip out of the operator's hand, it will not spin around and cause an injury. We always lowered sail with the handle off so that there would be no possibility of its striking us. The brake would be eased very gradually to control the sail's rate of descent. Once or twice the brake became a bit sticky from an accumulation of salt, and then I would clean it with a limited amount of fresh water.

The insidious enemy of the ocean sailor is chafe. The rubbing of lines and sails that normally causes no concern when sailing short distances can be serious on a long passage. It's especially important to prevent chafe aloft, as going to the masthead at sea is seldom easy. In former days, offshore boats were festooned with baggywrinkle, but I don't really think that is necessary nowadays, provided chafing strips are added to the sails where they touch the rigging. We had strips sewn on the mainsail near the luff where it lay against the after shrouds when the boom was broad off and also where the sail lay against the spreaders.

The Barient reel winch for the main halyard. The screw toggle brake allows hoisting with the brake on. Recently Barient added the following warnings to all of its reel winches: "Set brake before cranking" and "Remove handle before releasing brake."

Of course, the jibs had chafing patches where they touched the spreaders and life lines. Also, we used the boom vang a great deal to hold the boom steady and thus prevent the upper part of the main from rubbing against the rigging. As for running rigging, we tied off halyards, rigged chafe guards, and used shock-cord preventers to alleviate rubbing where necessary. I tried to make a habit of regular inspections of the rig for chafe, wear, or any potential problems.

At sea, my favorite points of sailing lie from close-hauled to a broad reach. Although I love to sail *Kelpie* hard on the wind, any passagemaker wants to be reasonably close to fetching his destination. The worst point of sailing is perhaps when the wind is just abaft the quarter, because this is when the headsail begins to be blanketed by the main, and the boat will often roll a great deal, because the sails lose their steadying power due to their being broad off. When on this point of sailing, we usually prefer either to sail a bit high of the course, or else to bear off a little so that the headsail can be boomed out. An important item on any cruising boat is a proper pole to boom out the jib. We used a standard spinnaker pole, which was only the length of the base of the fore triangle, and it could have been a bit longer. However, all of our jibs except the drifter-reacher had moderate foot lengths, so the pole served well enough.

As mentioned earlier, *Kelpie* was sailed very conservatively. We were not racing, and I did not want to drive the boat so hard as to scare Sally and Sarah (as well as myself). A couple of remarks from Sally's diary show clearly how she felt about our trying to make all possible speed. On June 10th, she wrote: "Stars really bright, but being on deck alone scary. Talked Jud out of shaking out our reefed main in the dark. I'm the chicken of the sea, and consequently we only made about three miles during my watch." Again on June 14th, she wrote: "I have a very uneasy feeling about Rip and Jud. Once racers always racers. I think they each have a subconscious goal to make good time on this run. I'm all for taking it easy even if it means a few extra days." Perhaps I did have a desire to put up more sail than we were carrying at certain times, but only because I hate to see any boat sailing inefficiently. My better judgment told me, however, that a conservative policy would be best for the boat and ourselves. I was especially concerned about being overburdened when Sarah and Sally were on watch alone at night; so we quite often shortened down just before dark if there seemed to be any chance of the wind piping up.

Of course, our conservatism was far more pronounced at the beginning of the passage, because it was then that we had the worst weather, and we gradually built up our confidence in night sailing as time went by. Then too, as our destination grew ever more close, there was a greater temptation to crowd on sail. An advertising folder of Fayal was tacked up over the chart table, and each day the pictures of that emerald isle looked more and more appealing. Near the end of the passage, Sally would take a wistful look at the folder and actually ask, "Can't we carry just a little more sail?"

11

COOKING AND MEALS
or
A Minor Miracle

If an army travels on its stomach, it could be said that a seaman does likewise. At least there is no doubt that proper food contributes a great deal to the welfare of the crew in terms of fitness, energy, and morale. Having been on a Bermuda race with a seasick cook, I can testify to the value of having the galley manned by someone who is not overly affected by the boat's motion. Sally felt a bit queasy occasionally, but she was almost always able to turn out good meals regardless, and if she didn't feel quite up to it, Rip and Sarah could fill in very well. I'm not completely helpless in the galley myself, although I'll have to confess that I've sometimes pretended to be in our kitchen at home.

In her role as chief cook and provisioner, Sally put a lot of preliminary thought into the planning of meals. With some help from Sarah, she made up 20 different dinner menus in order to simplify provisioning and to provide plenty of variety. The

Sally at work in the galley. Notice how the alcove and sturdy bulkhead post give the cook security in heavy weather.

following list shows the 10 most popular meals. All the main ingredients were canned (or bottled) unless otherwise noted.

(1) Beef with wine and pickle (a stew made with Wilson's roast beef, beef bouillon, sweet pickles) served with fresh potatoes and sprout salad.

(2) Sweet and sour ham (made with cubed ham, apricots, freeze-dried green peppers, chicken broth, vinegar, sugar, and soy sauce) served with chow mein noodles and fresh cole slaw.

(3) Chicken Niçoise (made with boneless chicken, artichoke hearts, pitted olives, garlic powder, Red Pack whole tomatoes, dry white wine, chicken broth, chopped tarragon) served with rice and fruit salad.

(4) Noodles and meat balls (made with noodles instead of spaghetti to save water, meat balls, and Sauce Arturo) served with Parmesan cheese, biscuits, and asparagus vinaigrette.

(5) Curried pork (made with Wilson's pork, raisins, cut-up fresh apples and onions, curry powder) served with rice and mandarin orange salad.

(6) Turkey stew (Wilson's turkey, fresh onions, and mushrooms) served with cranberry sauce, muffins, and garbanzo salad.

(7) Corned beef hash (cooked with dried onions and Sauce Arturo) served with grits and fresh Waldorf salad.

(8) Shrimp and artichoke casserole (made with Gulf Queen shrimp, artichokes, mushrooms, and Milani Newburg sauce) served with rice and sprout salad.

(9) Madame Durand's potato and eggs (made with fresh potatoes, onions, and eggs) served with biscuits, raw carrots, and palm heart and artichoke salad.

(10) Lobster rarebit (made with lobster, Welsh rarebit, mushrooms, and white wine) served with rice and avocado or sprout salad.

Another dish, which became a favorite after we had been eating canned foods for a long while, was a stew made from dried bouillon, fresh carrots, fresh onions, and fresh potatoes. Also, a great relief from a steady canned diet were the fresh salads mentioned in the list of meals. The Waldorf was our own modified version, consisting of carrots, apples, nuts, water chestnuts, and raisins. The sprout salad was especially well liked, and we ate these boat-grown greens in one form or another almost every day. A favorite form was to mix them with canned whole tomatoes and some raw onions dressed with oil and vinegar.

Many kinds of seeds (obtainable from a health food store) can be sprouted, such as cress, mustard, sunflower, and mung beans, but Sally preferred alfalfa. With three one-quart Mason jars, she could keep us adequately supplied every day. The jars were fitted with ventilated tops consisting of ordinary window screening cut to fit the standard screw-on ring tops. The sprouting procedure is as follows:

- Soak one tablespoon of alfalfa seed in a half cup of water in one of the jars.
- A day later, pour water off seeds (save for cooking). Put a quarter of a cup of water in the jar and swish gently to

A jar of sprouts. On this particular jar, the screen top is a plastic kind that can be obtained from a health food store or elsewhere, but tops made of ordinary window screening serve just as well.

rinse seeds. Pour off water (save). Turn the jar on its side with seeds distributed all around the jar. Place jar (on its side) on a galley counter out of the dark but not in direct sunlight.

- Repeat rinse about six to eight hours later and start second jar of alfalfa just as the first jar was started.
- The following day start the third jar. The second jar should be rinsed as previously described, and the first jar may have sprouts that are ready to eat. If not, rinse again and give the sprouts another day before eating them.

This process is continual so that new sprouts are available each day. We ate the seed hulls along with the sprouts, as they have an agreeable texture and are very nourishing. The seeds being sprouted should be kept damp but not soggy. This normally means that rinsing should be done twice a day, once in the morning and once in the evening. The soak and rinse water should be saved for cooking, not only to conserve drinking water, but also because it is very rich in vitamins and minerals. Incidentally, for cooking at sea, we used one-third sea water with two-thirds fresh, which included the sprout water. A device we didn't have but one that would have been useful is a rack designed to hold three sprout jars lying on their sides. We had to wedge our jars to keep them from rolling around.

After a cold night watch, we eagerly looked forward to breakfast. Our favorite menu was Dak's Danish bacon and fresh eggs, but sometimes we had oatmeal with milk, or a dish we all enjoyed, grits with bacon bits and butter. For lunches, we generally had sandwiches: tuna fish with sprouts and capers, Dak dried salami, grilled cheese, peanut butter, etc., and quite often we had soup: clam chowder, bouillon, vichyssoise, black bean with lemon, etc.

As a special treat, Sally would sometimes make blueberry muffins or biscuits. For these, she used an Optimus Mini-Oven that we bought from L. L. Bean. This is a small aluminum pot with iron bottom that is designed for roasting or baking on a stove top. Although our stove had its own large oven under the burners, Sally preferred to use the small Optimus oven at sea, because it was handier, less dangerous, and less wasteful of fuel.

In the important matter of liquid intake, we had plenty of soft drinks and beer. The former were consumed at a rather steady rate by Rip and Sarah. Sally and I normally preferred canned fruit juices, tea, coffee, and bouillon. A drink that was popular with everyone was Ellis energizer, named after a friend who gave us the recipe. This is a mixture of dried milk, creamer, Nestle's Quick (powdered chocolate), and powdered sugar. The drink is not only tasty and warming but also a real energy booster. Rip and I expected to consume a lot of beer, but we quickly found out it loses much appeal when warm. We did have one or two cocktails before dinner (my favorite was Mount Gay rum with water and lime juice), and quite often we had wine with meals.

Although fresh water must be used with care at sea, everyone on board *Kelpie* was encouraged to drink plenty, because a sailing doctor had told us it is very important for good health. We conserved the supply by using sea water for washing and to some extent for cooking, but there was no limit put on drinking water until after the first two weeks at sea when I became concerned about how long the passage was taking. After that, water was limited to half a gallon per person per day, but this is ample when there are other drinks on board. To begin with, all the water was measured in a graduated container so that we could tell how much was being used, but I'll have to admit we lost track after the first bout with heavy weather (there was a measuring port in the water tank but it was a bit difficult to get at). A fresh lemon was kept by the galley faucet so that we could squeeze some juice into the drinking water to give it a pleasant flavor and supply some vitamin C, which is needed to stave off scurvy. Of course, we also took vitamin pills.

As for cooking, we had three stoves, a primary and two back-ups. The primary was the three-burner alcohol HilleRange mentioned in Chapter 3. I also said that its gimballing was improved to about 35 degrees, and this made the stove almost perfect. It was always easy to light, did not produce fumes that were too objectionable, and was surprisingly economical. There were only one or two occasions, during the heaviest weather, when it could not be used. My only criticism of the stove is that certain parts are not made from rust-proof materials.

I had read warnings against alcohol stoves for long voyages because of their rapid consumption of fuel and the difficulty of obtaining good alcohol in foreign ports. That is primarily why we took the backup stoves, which were one-burner Sea Swings, one fueled with Sterno and the other with lamp oil (a good grade of kerosine). As it turned out, we never needed to use them, except for the Sterno model on rare occasions, because the HilleRange proved so easy to use and economical. We took about ten gallons of True Heat alcohol, which was more than enough for the passage over and back.

The kerosine stove was a Swedish Primus model that we obtained from A. B. Optimus, Inc., P.O. Box 907, La Mirada, California 90637. It came with a non-gimballed stand, but the stove is easily mounted on a standard Sea Swing gimbal that holds the burner level regardless of the vessel's motion or angle of heel. The Optimus company sells a special conversion kit for

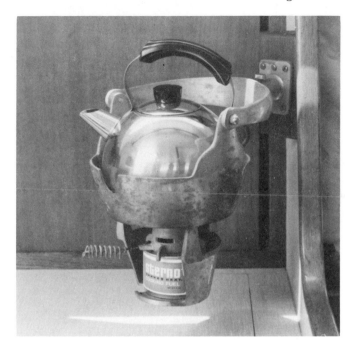

One of our two swing stoves for extra heavy weather or when one merely wants to heat a kettle of water for a hot drink.

the Sea Swing installation. I'll have to admit that at first we had problems keeping the stove lighted, but the people from Optimus couldn't have been more helpful or pleasant to deal with, and they supplied us with a complete spare parts kit.

Most of our pots and pans were kept in the ice box, since it was convenient to the stove and was not needed for food, although we did keep a few vegetables and soft drinks in one of its compartments. A nesting cookware set with Teflon-coated utensils of stainless steel proved quite adequate for most needs; but a few other pots and pans were all but indispensable. These included a pressure cooker for quickly cooking fresh vegetables, a kettle for boiling water quickly, a deep Revere Ware saucepan with a small bottom to fit in the Sea Swings, and a cast-iron skillet, which, in our opinion, has never been equalled for the

The after part of the galley, showing the cutting board that fits securely over the sink. The almost vital paper towels are hung in a convenient location just below the binoculars box.

likes of bacon and pancakes. Another utensil for which Sally found many uses was a plastic colander with a snap-on top.

Some other useful galley implements were: a wood cutting board with a slight rail that would fit securely over the sink to augment counter space, cooking tongs for picking up hot food, a large and a small knife of non-stainless steel that could be sharpened easily and would hold their edges, a heavy-duty portable can opener and a spare (ours were Swing-A-Ways), and a sheet of asbestos for taming the burner flames when cooking on very low heat and to protect the counter tops from hot pots. Sally used a sheet of Rubbermaid Shelf Kushion on the counter to keep pots and dishes from sliding around, and a pot holder made by HilleRange was most useful to keep the pressure

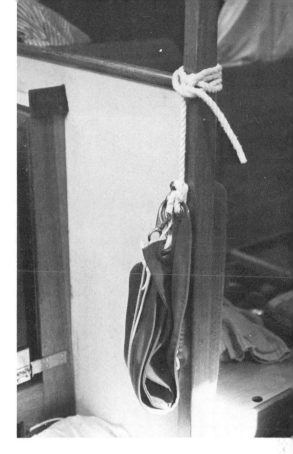

The cooking belt can be attached at two levels: at the eye strap on which it is hooked, so that one can sit on the belt, or at the higher level where the belt support line is tied around the post for greater security.

cooker and other pots steady on the stove. Our plates and mugs, made by Yachting Tableware Co., were the kind that have rubber rings on the bottom, and they were all but essential in heavy weather.

I've already told about our double-strap cooking belt. This is not only important to prevent being thrown into or away from the stove in heavy weather, but also it allows the cook to use both hands at all times. Our belt was quite satisfactory, but it could have been a little more heavily made, as it began to show signs of wear before the cruise was over. Another important piece of equipment for cooking in rough seas is a long, waterproof apron for protection against the spilling of hot foods. Sally made one of light-weight rubberized cloth.

The quality of meals on a small boat at sea obviously depends to a large extent on the state of the weather. When the boat is trying to stand on her head or is bucking like a bronco, elaborate cooking is too difficult; and if the crew are half seasick, they don't feel like eating anyway. However, every effort should be made to provide something hot and palatable, because it is so important to the crew's welfare, both physically and mentally.

The meals were not always gourmet on *Kelpie*, but they were nutritionally balanced, and we always ate something, even in the worst weather. Fortunately, we were able to keep our health. There were no digestive problems, and no one lost much weight. In fact, Sally gained some. To me, food on a boat always tastes a little better than it does on shore, and a first-class meal at sea always seems like a minor miracle.

12

HEAVY WEATHER

or

She Knows Better What to Do Than You

The gale we experienced on June 20th and 21st was certainly not what I would call survival weather (although the rest of the crew might disagree), but it was most impressive. Now that it is all over with, I'm glad to have had the first-hand experience, but I don't want it again. Sally thought she saw, to her complete irritation, a look of exaltation on my face during the height of the blow. What she actually saw was a look of awe mixed with fright; but nonetheless, I'll have to admit that I found the gale extremely interesting, even if I disliked it.

The wind was somewhat frightening because of its deafening scream, but it was not doing us any real harm (except for some chafe) when we were under bare pole. In fact, pressure from the wind helped steady the boat and prevent her from rolling to weather when we lay ahull. What really concerned us. however, were the seas, because they were so steep and confused. I cannot say just how high they were, but they seemed almost as high as the spreaders when we lay in the trough.

John Letcher holds with the theory, which he expounded at the 1977 Chesapeake Sailing Yacht Symposium, that sailors often exaggerate the size of waves when running before following seas because of a disoriented frame of reference. With the boat on a wave slope, the sailor thinks of his deck as being horizontal, and this makes the wave ahead appear much larger than it really is (see Figure 12-1). In our case, however, we were lying broadside to the seas and were moderately heeled, even in the trough, from the wind pressure on the rigging. If we had felt that our deck was horizontal, the apparent height of the waves to windward would have been smaller than the actual height (as shown in Figure 12-1). Thus, I think we can say that the waves were high without too much concern about exaggeration. Furthermore, they were surprisingly short for midocean waves, and this was probably due to the approximate 120-degree shift of wind after the front came through. Then too, we were in the Gulf Stream and the current probably added to the state of sea confusion after the wind shift.

Our friend Fred Davis, who is the chief meteorologist at Baltimore-Washington International Airport, very kindly supplied us with synoptic charts from the National Weather Service covering the period of our cruise. The surface charts during the time of the big gale are most interesting, although they are rather puzzling in some respects. On June 19th, a major depression was passing over Newfoundland. A warm front from the center of the low extended to the southeast, while a cold front extended west southwestward from the center. At 0800 (our time) on the 20th, a small kink or wave began to form in the cold front, which ran in a slightly more southwesterly direction on the left side of the kink. By 2000, a small secondary low formed to the northeast of us, its center being in the approximate location of 43°30' north latitude and 51° west longitude. During the night, the front passed over us, and we experienced the dramatic shift of wind from southwesterly to northerly directions.

The synoptic chart for 0200 on the 21st shows the front having passed over us and the low developing with its center moving to about 44° north and 48° west. The depression

URE 12-1: APPARENT WAVE HEIGHT

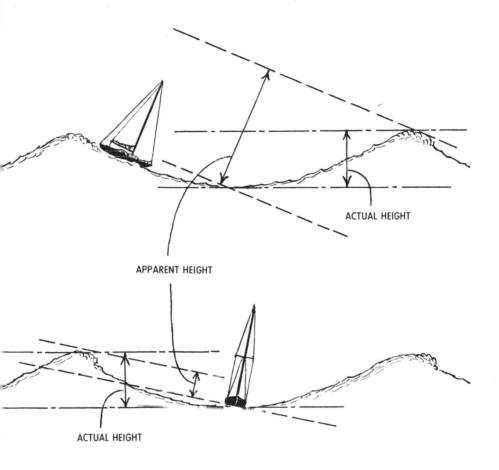

ACTUAL HEIGHT

APPARENT HEIGHT

ACTUAL HEIGHT

matured, and curiously enough, it turned about-face and headed southwest so rapidly that the 0800 position of its center was located about 40° north and 55° west. Our approximate position at that time was 39° north and 57° west. Six hours later, the low had deepened, its center moved to the west about 2½ degrees, and we began to experience our strongest wind, which blew from a bit east of north. This situation is illustrated in Figure 13-2, and it can be seen that *Kelpie* was very close to

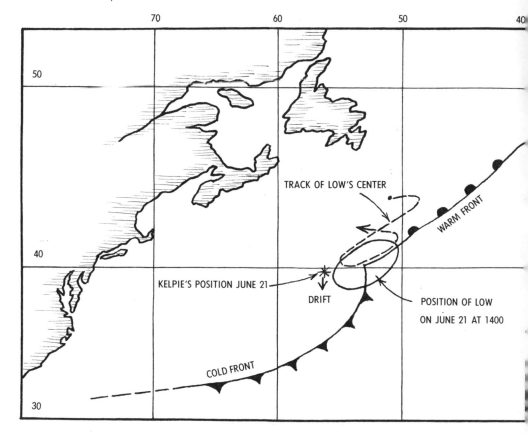

FIGURE 12-2: BEGINNING OF THE HARDEST BLOW

the isobar of lowest pressure. Our barometer read 29.5 inches, but I'm not sure how accurate it was with the boat's motion being so violent.

Subsequent synoptic charts show the track of the center of the low making a completely closed loop. It is difficult to explain this erratic behavior of the secondary low. Fred Davis feels that the low should have moved along the front from west to east, and he says that the synoptic plots are often unreliable because they are based on reports (possibly inaccurate) from only a few scattered ships. On the other hand, there are occasional lows that behave most erratically, twisting, curving, and hooking. Did I hear a meteorologist calling them hookers, or am I becoming a dirty old man?

Adlard Coles, in his book *Heavy Weather Sailing*, described a Gulf Stream storm that made a complete loop north of Bermuda in 1950. U.S. and British meteorologists were in wide disagreement concerning the track of the low, but they did agree that it must have made a loop. It seems that accurate conclusions regarding midocean storms cannot always be drawn from weather charts and radio reports. The offshore sailor only knows what he experiences, and even his recollections may lack reliability unless careful, objective notes are kept during the experience.

As for boat management in storms at sea, I have already mentioned in Chapter 7 that during the worst of the weather we experienced, I felt we had a choice of two alternatives: (1) to run off under the tiny spitfire jib (sheeted flat) towing drags (the tire) or (2) to lie ahull, a tactic whereby the helm is abandoned and the boat is allowed to drift freely with all sails down. Most boats will naturally assume a beam-on or slightly stern-up position when hulling, and it is customary to lash the helm down (rudder to windward) to keep the boat beam-on and inhibit headway. After some deliberation, we decided on the second alternative.

Immediately prior to lying ahull, we had been scudding under bare pole, because it was blowing too hard for heaving to under storm sails. But running off, *Kelpie* was going too fast; she was becoming unmanageable (tending to broach to); and occasional seas were breaking over her stern. We had the tiny spitfire with an area of only 42 square feet, and I figured that if we hoisted it and sheeted it flat, it would help hold the bow off and lessen the tendency to broach, but on the other hand, the sail would increase our speed. Drags towed astern might have helped slow the speed, but they would have hampered steering in much the same way that a vessel being towed affects the steering of the towboat, unless there is a towing bitt far forward near the towboat's turning axis, as on a tug. Another consideration was that

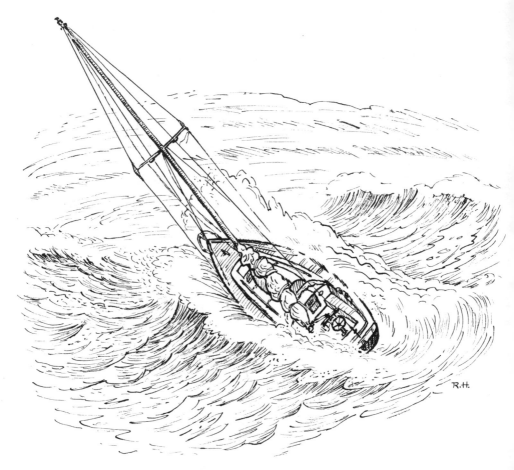

LYING AHULL IN THE HEAVY GALE

the weather was so bad I didn't want anyone to go forward to set the storm jib, and it would have been difficult rigging the drags. Furthermore, Rip and I were becoming fatigued fighting the helm, and, male chauvinist pig that I am, I did not want Sarah or Sally to take their tricks at the helm in those conditions.

Lying ahull seemed the preferable tactic, because it required little or no effort, no one needed to be on deck, and *Kelpie* seemed to be well suited for hulling. This suitability is largely due to her low center of gravity and therefore high resistance to capsizing and considerable ability to self-right. In addition, she has the kind of configuration under water that allows a high degree of leeway when there is little forward speed, and this means that she can yield to the smash of seas without tripping. Also, she has reinforced round bilges and a sturdy cabin trunk with windows that are not excessively large, and all of these features are helpful when it comes to exposing the beam to the wind and seas. A further argument for hulling was that *Kelpie* had been taking some water over the stern when running off, but a beam-on position would provide maximum buoyancy.

Despite these reasons and the fact that I had heard of many successful hulling experiences, it was terribly difficult in a psychological sense to turn the boat broadside to the elements and to abandon the helm. My natural instinct made me shrink from such an action, because I sensed that *Kelpie* would roll and perhaps be knocked down or battered by the confused seas, many of which had awesome breaking tops. I realized that there is always a possibility of capsizing in any boat. Nevertheless, I remembered the words of the great Thomas Fleming Day, whom I had quoted only a few years before in my book *Sea Sense*. Captain Day, famous editor of *The Rudder* magazine and promoter of ocean sailing for small yachts, wrote as follows: "My long experience in small boats has taught me this: that if a boat is a good boat, when real trouble comes she is best let alone. She knows better what to do than you, and if you leave her alone, she will do the right thing; whereas nine times out of ten you will do the wrong."

With Captain Day's words in my mind and a feeling of confidence that *Kelpie* was a good boat, I told Rip, who was then steering, to put the helm down and bring the bow up. He waited for a relative smooth in the seas and let the bow come up so that the wind was on the starboard beam. Then we secured the helm down (rudder to windward) with the wheel's locking screw. *Kelpie* heeled to port, and I expected all hell to break loose, but to my surprise she rode the waves like the stormy petrels that were sitting on the water near us. A frightening sea with breaking crest would rush at our side, but *Kelpie* would lean away and skid off to leeward at an unexpected rate, avoid-

Rip at the helm staring in awe at a large breaking sea.

ing the full impact of the smash. At times, when on the crest of a sea, it seemed as though *Kelpie* were going to be pushed off a cliff of water and rolled or dropped on her side into the trough, yet somehow she stayed on her feet and never landed as hard as expected. To be sure, there was some violent motion, and it was necessary to hang on every minute, but seas were no longer breaking into the cockpit and our forward speed through the water almost stopped. At any rate, it was a relief being able to go below into the warmth and apparent security of the cabin.

For about the first hour after all of us were below, we were a bit anxious, not knowing how *Kelpie* would behave when left on her own in such a seaway; but then we began to get confidence that she could fend for herself without our help. Of course, I still had some concern that we could be hit by a freak sea that might roll us over or crush the cabin trunk, but the odds seemed to be against this. *Kelpie* lay about broadside to the elements, although she did some switching around and exposed her stern to the seas on occasions. Once in a while a sea would break under her counter and make the whole boat vibrate. In retrospect, I think we should have lashed the helm down with shock cord rather than relying on the lock screw, which I think was slipping and allowing the rudder to change position. Of course, having the rudder held to windward helped keep the boat beam-on to the seas for maximum buoyancy and minimum forward speed, which is what we wanted in those conditions.

As I said in Chapter 7, it was much quieter in the cabin than on deck; yet certain sounds were louder: the smash of seas against the topsides, the creaking of bulkheads, and heavy spray striking the dinghy which made it resound like a kettle drum. I was somewhat concerned about the bulkheads moving, as I have actually seen this happen on other boats in better weather, but *Kelpie's* did not move. Most of the creaking seemed to come from the top edge where the main bulkhead was butted against the cabin top. Also, there was some complaining in way of the foul-weather-gear locker. At one point I tried a test that I recall was suggested by the well-known seaman Rod Stephens. I repeatedly opened and closed all doors to see if they were sticking, which might indicate that the hull or deck were changing shape, but no sticking could be detected anywhere.

Although the windows were struck hard many times, the topsides and bottom were taking the brunt, and I think that for the most part only hard-driven sheets of spray were hitting the plexiglass. Also, the weather cloths were taking a lot of the force and were giving some protection to the windows and dinghy as well. The stanchions that supported the weather cloths were bent inboard somewhat, but that was a minor consideration, and it is not very difficult to bend the stanchions back to their normal position. Incidentally, there should be a large space under the weather cloths so that water on the deck can run overboard.

Our hulling experience, which lasted for 15 hours on the 21st and 22nd of June, gave us a good deal of confidence in the tactic, and it made real believers of us in regard to certain requirements below deck. Proper, strongly made bunk boards or lee cloths are a must. Also, there should be adequate hand grips, and all edges and corners must be well rounded. Sally was thrown hard against the corner of the chart table, and I'm convinced she would have been badly hurt if the corner had not been round. It is all but essential to have a large-capacity, preferably permanent bilge pump in the cabin. We had to pump quite often because of the leak through the rudder shaft. Sturdy storm slides are also a must, and I had confidence in ours, which were described earlier, but I now think we could have used a latch on the small, outward-swinging window in the top slide in the event that *Kelpie* were rolled upside down. Needless to say, all objects below must be well secured so that they cannot break loose in a knockdown or rollover.

It is desirable to have small, sturdy windows or ports around the entire cabin trunk for lookout purposes. *Kelpie* has two ports and two small windows forward in the sides of the trunk but none on the forward-facing end, which would have helped visibility somewhat. During the night of the big gale, we didn't worry too much about being run down, because there seemed to be matters of greater concern. We simply turned on our spreader lights and trusted to providence that we would not be run down. Two nights later, however, when we lay ahull again in less boisterous conditions, I became somewhat uneasy at leaving the boat unwatched; so we stood our regular watches below deck, periodically peering out of the windows.

In our case, lying ahull seemed to be the right thing to do, but that doesn't necessarily mean I would recommend it for every boat in every circumstance. There might be considerable risk in hulling for boats that can easily capsize and are deficient in the ability to self-right, especially when breaking waves have plunging rather than spilling tops. Spillers are usually seen on deep water waves, while plunging breakers often occur in shoal water (even water over the continental shelves) or when the wind opposes a strong current. We had a few plungers, probably resulting from the abrupt wind shift and the effect of current, but I felt *Kelpie* had ample reserve stability to right promptly even if she were rolled over, and I believed her decks and cabin trunk were sufficiently strong to withstand heavy seas breaking aboard. Actually, little solid water was dumped squarely on deck because of *Kelpie*'s considerable angle of heel and her rapid leeway. Furthermore, her drift wake to windward seemed to encourage most seas to break before they reached the hull.

Although some experienced sailors do not think lying ahull is advisable in the very heaviest weather, there are arguments for this tactic even during extreme conditions, because there are many cases of derelict boats surviving after having been abandoned during storms. Even though the crews had abandoned because they felt sinking was imminent, the derelicts were found days later after having been through the worst kind of weather.

Hal Roth, author of *After 50,000 Miles*, is opposed to hulling in extreme conditions, and he cites the example of the Contest 31 sloop *Banjo*, which was abandoned near Bermuda after she had been damaged by a hurricane while lying ahull in 1975. In this particular case, however, I think that construction more than tactics should be blamed, because *Banjo* had a vulnerable skeg that caused a crack in the boat's bottom after she dropped into a trough. In the words of a crew member, "The skeg obviously bent beyond the rupture point because the crack appeared along the seam between the skeg and the hull." Deep, narrow skegs are often vulnerable, and more than a few boats with this feature have had serious problems at sea. Roth states that he knows of a dozen cases of boats in trouble from lying ahull, but by the same token, I could name a dozen or more boats that came to grief while running off, the tactic advocated by Roth in severe storms.

There is at least one great comfort for small boat sailors in midocean during heavy weather: they do not have to worry about running out of sea room. Along a coast, you must be concerned about being caught on a lee shore. If a severe storm prevents you from clawing off and forces you to scud (run off) in the direction of shore or even to lie ahull, a sea anchor must be used. Sea anchors can impose terrible strains and may overly tether or hold a boat too securely so that she cannot give to the seas. Furthermore, most modern yachts, on account of their windage forward and underwater shape, cannot be made to lie head-to-wind with a sea anchor streamed from the bow. We had two cornucopia drogues and a tire (see Chapter 5) but never had to use them, because it was never necessary to slow our drift. We drifted about 30 miles during the 15 hours of lying ahull.

During the height of our heaviest weather on the afternoon of June 21st, the storm seemed interminable, and had we been anywhere near the land, I would have been worried to death. Of course we had some anxieties and a strong feeling of isolation and naked exposure to the elements, but I remember thinking out loud, "Thank God for a decent offing; we have sea room to spare."

13

HUMAN RELATIONS
or
From Fogies to Folk

After our passage many of our friends and acquaintances have shown a great interest in the psychological aspects of the trip. They want to know about our emotions: fears, anxieties, pleasures, and how we got along with each other being cooped up for a month on a small boat. Many of our non-sailor friends seem to think that we were either very brave or else completely crazy (mostly the latter).

To begin with, I want to re-emphasize that I don't think what we did was anything special. Dozens and dozens of voyages much more spectacular and hazardous than ours are being made every year. However, our trip was a great adventure *for us*. And I'll have to admit in all honesty that we all are just a little bit proud that we made the trip and did it *en famille*, without any expert crew, and that we went through the big gale without any panic. I was much more proud of my family than I was of myself during the storm, because I had confidence in the boat, but Sally and Sarah were quite sure we were not going to

160

The crew of Kelpie *shortly after the cruise. Rip still wears the beard that he grew during the passage. (Mitch Kuhan)*

survive, while Rip seemed a bit dubious. I was apprehensive, but only over the possibility of rolling over, losing the mast, or one of us becoming injured. I never really feared that we would founder, although I had a real concern about one of us going overboard. At any rate, we were all pleased at the way we came through the experience and felt that we passed a kind of personal character test. It was once written in the Slocum Society's journal, *The Spray*, that "One gale will tell us more about ourselves than years on the psychiatrist's couch." There is certainly some truth in that.

I had read and even written about the offshore sailor's point of no return (PNR), when he feels there is no turning back, that it is far more difficult to turn back than to continue a passage. This can be a critical mental period for some sailors, as they may feel they have severed their last link with home. Of course, the feeling may only apply to shorthanded or solo sailing, because sailors with limited responsibilities on fully crewed vessels may not think they have full control over their destinies.

On *Kelpie*, we jokingly called our PNR feelings the UC (umbilical cord). Sally had a strong sense of being attached to home by our daily, dead-reckoning positions. She felt that we could retrace our steps as long as we knew where we were. It was almost as though we could pull ourselves back by the line that was drawn on our chart. Her UC period of mental stress came immediately after the big gale when we lost track of our DR. At that time, she did not have confidence in our celestial navigation, and she felt we were lost, even though we could not have been more than about 30 to 40 miles away from our last DR position.

I suppose my own UC was also related to the navigation, because it was my responsibility, and I was somewhat disturbed by the discrepancies between the DR and celestial positions. However, my real point of no return came early, when the shores of New Jersey dropped below the horizon, because turning back after that for no good reason would have been too humiliating. I think Rip felt very much the same way.

Sarah's UC was associated with the radio. She has always loved music, and she got great comfort from listening to the radio. It was a real link with home. She was allowed the use of an old Zenith Royal 790 Super Navigator, and I could really write a testimonial for this radio, as it was on deck almost every night during Sarah's watch except in the very worst weather. It was knocked around and often drenched with salt spray, but it never failed and the only trouble we had was with corroded battery terminals, which were easy to clean. From my quarter berth that runs under the starboard cockpit seat, I could hear the radio during Sarah's watch, and I vividly remember two songs being played repeatedly, *Love Will Keep Us Together* by

Captain and Tennille and *Wildfire* by Michael Murphy. Whenever I hear these tunes today, they bring back a flood of memories, especially the flute-like passages in *Wildfire*. Of course, the further we progressed on our cruise, the fainter became the radio signals from home until they faded away entirely. Sarah's UC was stretched thin until it finally broke. Actually, we could receive U.S. stations all the way across on our Zenith Trans-oceanic, but that radio was important for time signals, weather reports, and a standby RDF, so we didn't use it for music. Eventually, of course, Sarah began to pick up European stations, and this afforded some comfort, but the link with home was gone.

A voyage is full of emotional ups and downs, and not surprisingly, the offshore sailor's feelings are greatly affected by the weather. I don't think any of us realized, however, the full extent to which our emotions would be ruled by the elements. A beautiful, sunny day would be pure joy, and our spirits would soar, but cold, wet weather could be most depressing. It almost seemed that our spirits were linked to the barometer. Of course, the strength and direction of the wind would very much affect our attitude. A good sailing breeze that sped us toward our destination would give us a tremendous emotional high; but an increasing blow that meant rough seas, discomfort, and difficult sail changes could be utterly loathsome; while long periods of calm weather with swells that rolled the boat and slatted her sails could produce extreme impatience and irritation. I doubt if many landsmen realize the degree of affinity with the elements the offshore sailor feels. We found ourselves constantly attuned to the sea and sky, forever studying the waves and clouds. They meant the difference between extreme pleasure and perhaps considerable discomfort or annoyance, even apprehension.

When we were emotionally down, it was helpful if just one of us could remain somewhat cheerful and optimistic. A little joke, pun, or lightheartedness from one of us could help buck up the spirits of all. The cultivation of humor, even in a base form, is valuable during hard times. I remember how we laughed during one of the moderate gales when "Mom" went below to the head and came up on deck with the pumping instructions stuck to the seat of her trousers. Evidently, she had been thrown against the bulkhead on which the instructions were posted, and they stuck to her seat. The incident gave our morale a much-needed lift.

During disagreeable weather, the smallest little comfort could cheer us up. A cup of hot soup, for instance, or a bit of fresh food to go along with a canned meal would make a world of difference in our outlook. Comfort items that we considered almost vital in rough weather were the weather cloths and cockpit dodger, while the helmsman's chair and awning were a great help when it was hot and calm.

A great boost to the morale is a proper bunk. At the outset, we agreed that everyone should have his own berth with an adjacent locker or two for clothes and personal gear. This area would be one's own private home, so to speak. Fortunately, *Kelpie*'s layout provided four good bunks aft near the center of rotation to minimize the motion caused by pitching, but the bunks were not all equally attractive. Sally was given the most comfortable bunk, which was the dinette area filled in. It was

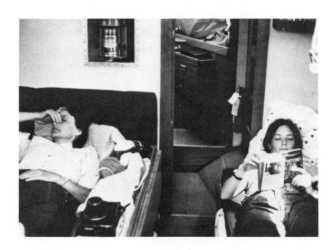

Sally and Sarah relaxing on their bunks. Sarah, on the starboard side, does not have her lee cloth up, since it is a calm day. The large metal object on the bulkhead behind Sally is the charcoal heating stove.

easy to get into and the adjacent drop leaf table made a natural bunk board, but the berth was a little too wide for extremely heavy weather when the boat was rolling. Rip's bunk was an upper pilot berth that required some acrobatic ability when climbing in or out, because I insisted that a substantial lee cloth be rigged all the time in order to assure that Rip could never be thrown out by a sudden roll or knockdown.

Sarah and I alternated between the quarter berth and sliding transom seat. The latter was really Sarah's assigned bunk, but she preferred the quarter berth, which was my assigned bunk, because it was out of the way of traffic, was darker, and needed no lee cloth. It is interesting that Sarah and I both preferred the quarter berth, and we liked to go into it head first, while Rip and Sally found that way of sleeping claustrophobic. I found the foot of the quarter berth narrow enough to easily brace myself when the boat was rolling; and perhaps in heavy weather Sarah and I subconsciously felt the location afforded some degree of protection, a sort of return-to-the-womb complex.

In addition to our four berths aft, we had a spare bunk forward. This one was a bit too bouncy to use in rough seas, but we felt it was good to have as a kind of sanctum in fair weather. The forward cabin had a door, and it was the place to go when one wanted to escape temporarily and be alone. When living in crowded conditions, it is a big help to have some kind of private retreat, although Sarah claimed she learned the trick of mental detachment to such an extent that she could be alone within herself.

I don't mean to imply that conditions on the boat were often unpleasant. Most of the time we very much enjoyed the company of each other, and we were seldom, if ever, bored. In fact, we were very often excited or thrilled with our experience. Sally got a great emotional lift from being in a pristine pure environment where there was no pollution whatsoever. In mid-ocean on a sailboat the air is unbelievably clean, and there is a blissful absence of man-made noise and industrial odors. The water is so clear that on a sunny day you can see light rays penetrating more than 30 feet below the surface. Contrary to what Thor Heyerdahl reported in lower latitudes during his *Ra* voyage, we saw almost no garbage floating in the sea, except for occasional patches of plastic foamed "peanuts" used in commercial packing. Those small plastic particles became trapped in the numerous tide rips we saw south of Newfoundland, and eventually, I suppose, they end up in the Sargasso Sea.

Rip was particularly taken with the many spectacular sunsets seen through unpolluted air and with a 360-degree horizon. He took numerous photos of the sun seeming to extinguish itself in the sea. I was equally impressed with the dawns during my trick at the helm and I always felt a kind of gratitude, like a primitive man, for the warmth and light of the rising sun. Sarah felt a great kinship with the stars and planets. She is no astrologist, but some of her friends show a tongue-in-cheek interest in the subject, and apparently there was some significance that Mars and Jupiter were in conjunction during the middle of our passage. At any rate, all of us became quite intimate with the sky and its celestial bodies after being on watch for 26 consecutive nights. Of course, the period when we had a full moon and when we could almost sail up its silvery, reflected path was a time of pure joy.

Those night watches were sometimes tedious and unpleasant in foul weather, but quite often they were most rewarding, not only because of the chance to commune with nature, but because of the rare opportunity to reflect and meditate. I think Rip expressed this so well, when on June 29th he wrote in his diary: "The mental exercises that go on during a watch can be amazing. Some days or nights during watch I will sit at the helm feeling totally without thought and will amuse myself by looking at the great swaths of foam that go by or the clouds in the sky or the moon. Tonight was different. My mind was filled with memories and I seemed to relive past experiences vividly. I was in Maine picking raspberries, smelling the pine trees, and feeling the fog roll in; I was back in college going over the faces of my friends, their names, and little vignettes that for no real reason stuck in my mind; and then I was back at Gibson Island, going from one house to another, remembering the people who lived there. It was an interesting exercise in working on the old memory cells. It struck me as interesting to think that for years I hadn't thought so many thoughts or remembered so many little bits of my past life at any one time; and I wondered why. Perhaps, because modern man has so little time to cogitate his past, because he is so inescapably locked into his present—How much can I get done today? What have I accomplished? Is it enough? Can I sit idle for two hours and do nothing but think? I certainly feel that is true in my case. Being in New York, my energy has been burning along at a fever pitch. What little time there is left for relaxation is lazed away on T.V., light reading, or sleeping. So in conclusion, I feel those enforced periods of thinking on watch are a good thing. Man needs to reflect on his past and refresh those brain cells that hold his memories. Otherwise, they would pass away. I felt better after my two-hour watch, a bit drained but more of a person, appreciating what went before and realizing all that is what makes me the person I am."

The day-by-day rewards of a long ocean passage are many, but undoubtedly the greatest emotional high for all of us came when we made our landfall on the small island of Flores. As I mentioned in Chapter 9, the landfall was particularly thrilling for me, being a novice navigator and especially so because of the overcast skies that for two days previously had limited celestial observations. I had been able to get two somewhat indistinct sun sights through hazy breaks in the sky and obtain a running fix during the morning of July 4th, and soon after our position was plotted, the island "miraculously" appeared exactly where it should have been. At first it looked like a bank of clouds, but when it did not move, in contrast to the real clouds, we knew it was our destination. Seeing a tiny speck of land one is seeking rise up out of the vast ocean after weeks at sea is always a joy even for an experienced navigator, but for me that moment provided a thrill I'll not soon forget.

Strangely enough, some of the pleasurable moments offshore are blended with times of anxiety. During the big gale, for instance, there was an awesome beauty about the sea. It was especially spectacular when we passed into a relative lull near the center of the storm and the sun broke through the black overcast to light up the wild, tumbling water. The entire surface was a rich indigo streaked with creamy foam, but when the waves broke, they'd leave large patches of pale, swimming-pool turquoise that would linger for what seemed like minutes before fading away into the darker blue. As Sarah wrote in her diary, "Looking at those waves, I was fascinated by the piercing blue that shone as they almost engulfed us. Such a pretty color for something so deadly."

The sea life provided another mixture of apprehension and pleasure. All of us are nature and animal lovers, and we abhor the commercial slaughter of whales, but for some years I've been collecting reports of boats being damaged or sunk by sea life, and my list is quite impressive. Unfortunately, I made the mistake of showing that list to Sally before we left home, and she developed a real fear of whales. She had plenty of opportunities to be afraid, too, because we saw many whales, and they most often appeared when she was on watch alone. One day, while I was attending to my navigation chores below, I heard Sally stammering, "Whales—big whales!" I rushed up the companionway in time to see a large whale, about the size of *Kelpie* (a right whale, we think), leap entirely out of water just astern. Fortunately, the creatures left us alone and soon disappeared, but Sally was a bit unnerved. She said she had passed through a whole pod and had actually been wet by one of them blowing.

We had a number of visits from small pilot whales. They loved to follow in our wake, seeming to cavort and gambol in the most playful way. Sally was afraid they would hit the boat, and I was concerned they would carry away the taffrail log rotator, but they gave us no trouble and were a delight to watch. At night you could sometimes hear them astern. They would communicate with squeaking sounds and make popping noises, like large air bubbles rising to the surface of the water. Once we had become accustomed to the pilot whales, we lost our apprehensions and really looked forward to their company. "I've gotten so I'm no longer afraid of them," wrote Rip; "they seem so friendly and almost cute."

Maurice and Maralyn Bailey, the couple mentioned earlier who spent 118 days in a raft after their boat had been sunk by a wounded cachalot, became fascinated with whales after their ordeal, and they made quite a study of the creatures. Maurice told me that he didn't believe a whale would deliberately attack a boat unless there was a collision, and/or the whale was wounded, or the boat got between a cow and her calf.

During our trip, I had the same sort of gut feeling that we would not be molested by whales unless they were provoked, but I felt much less secure about killer whales. They seemed very unpredictable, and I distrusted them. Perhaps this concern was due to my reading of experiences like the one suffered by Dougal Robertson, whose boat was sunk by a pack of killer whales. We did not see many of these creatures, but one day we saw a group of them chasing a school of porpoises. Sally had done some reading about killer whales and subscribed to the theory that people on small boats should stay out of their sight, as the killer whales might mistake them for edible seals or penguins. I tried to comfort Sally by assuring her that I would not don my tuxedo and thereby run the risk of being mistaken for a penguin.

Of course, we saw other forms of sea life that were more a source of fascination than apprehension. These were dolphins, porpoises, a few flying fish (we were too far north to see a lot), occasional sea turtles and rays, numerous Portuguese men-of-war with their bubble sails thrust above the water, and we even saw a dead octopus or squid floating on the surface. Pelagic birds such as shearwaters, fulmars, petrels, and even frigate birds were often present, and we thoroughly enjoyed their company. But it was a bit frightening to see the Mother Carey's chickens (stormy petrels) sitting on the water during the bad gales, for they are said to do that only in the heaviest weather. Although the ocean is sometimes thought of as being a barren wasteland, we all had strong feelings, especially Sally, that the waters were positively teeming with life.

Our shipboard pets were the pigeon described in Chapter 7, and, for the first part of the passage, a spider named "Sea Legs" that lived for a surprisingly long time without adequate food. It

Our shipboard pet, Harry Pidgeon, on a cushion just outside his pigeon hole.

occupied the stern pulpit, and we could almost forecast the wind velocity by the size and density of its web. Before heavy weather it would seem to shorten sail. In Chapter 7, I mentioned "Mac the Knife," the large shark that persistently followed us for three days during our first gale. It was a bit disconcerting seeing his fin astern, rather like being tracked by a wolf or having vultures circling overhead, but fortunately none of us had, at the time, seen the movie *Jaws.*

I, personally, did not worry too much about dangerous sea life, but I did have occasional qualms about one of us becoming ill or having an accident, collisions with flotsam, and gear failure. Concerning the latter, I was amused before our trip by a conversation between Sally and a girl friend who was new to the sailing game. The girl's husband had just bought a new boat, and she was nervously inquiring about what to expect. "What is your greatest worry when sailing?" she asked. "Gear failure," Sally replied. The girl breathed a sigh of relief and said, "Thank goodness we don't have one of those on our boat."

Sally knew how equipment can fail, and this did give her, as well as me, some concern. We were somewhat comforted, however, by the fact that we had reputedly reliable fittings, and they were thoroughly inspected before we left. In addition, during the trip Rip or I made a daily check of gear that could be readily examined. We had Sally to thank for prodding us into going forward to inspect every turnbuckle and cotter pin even when the weather was foul. Of course, we were also comforted by the fact that we carried many spare parts and had given prior thought to jury rigs for some of the more common kinds of mishaps (see Chapter 3).

As for the possibility of illness or accidents, we reduced this worry by being medically prepared as well as possible and by being extremely conscious of safety. We used our safety belts and harnesses; moved about the boat and used the stove cautiously in heavy weather; and adhered to strict safety rules concerning the wearing of flotation jackets, carrying a pocket strobe light, and not leaving the cockpit at night unless there was another person on deck. Our medical supplies and preparations were described in Chapter 4. I felt we were quite well prepared, but it gives one a slightly uneasy feeling to think how isolated you are in the middle of the ocean. Of course, the emergency radios afforded some comfort in that we felt (perhaps rationalized) that help could be obtained reasonably soon in the event of a serious illness. A thorough physical examination before embarking is also reassuring.

My concern about colliding with flotsam stemmed from the fact that I had heard of several boats having been damaged or sunk from this cause. Also, Sally and I are regular readers of the monthly *Notice to Mariners*, which so often reports dangerous flotsam, such as logs, buoys, wreckage, oil drums, or containers, drifting offshore. Sarah was also concerned about this (even though she did not know about those frightening reports), because she had the feeling of "rushing into the unknown" when it was especially dark at night. Actually, this feeling only occurred early in the trip, because she eventually grew accustomed to her night watches. Our worries were alleviated by knowing that we had a strong, well-built boat, and I was consoled that she had a swept forefoot (Chapter 2) so that she would tend to ride up on any sizable object lying awash on or just below the surface.

I was proud of Sally and Rip on the cruise, and I was especially pleased with the behavior of Sarah, because she was the least experienced, and she really didn't know what she was

Sarah learned to steer a steady compass course even in difficult quartering seas.

getting into. The night watches during the first few days at sea must have been quite unpleasant, even frightening, for her when she was entirely alone on deck, particularly during a dark night when it was rough and windy. Then too, she lacked confidence in herself early in the passage and often felt a bit seasick. But she never really complained, and she never missed a watch except during the big gale when I wouldn't let her go on deck. Sarah's watch always followed mine, and very often in difficult conditions, I would stay with her for a while before I went below to be sure she had settled down, had the feel of the boat, and felt in her own mind that she could handle the situation. Toward the middle of the trip, Sarah developed into a fine "helmsman" and was steering better compass courses than I.

The best advice that could be given in the matter of obtaining crew for a long passage would emphasize choosing with care. Be sure you really know your crew before casting off. It is often a wise plan to take a short shake-down cruise to test the people as well as the boat before embarking on a voyage of any length. It is sometimes surprising how people will act when on board a small boat far offshore. I have heard stories of crew being completely incapacitated by seasickness, of their refusing to work, and even of their panicking and becoming completely irrational in heavy weather. Important qualities to look for are resistance to seasickness, sailing experience (preferably offshore), dependability, and congeniality. Think twice about picking a crew member who is accident-prone or one who lacks a sense of humor.

Family members do not always make the best crew, but in our case the arrangement was a happy one. We were a close family before we left, and we grew a lot closer before making our landfall. Sharing the experience developed a true camaraderie, mutual respect, and tolerance of each other. It did much to close the generation gap; for Sally and I now feel more like peers than parents, while our progenies now consider us more like folk than fogies.

14

LESSONS LEARNED
AND CONCLUSIONS
or
"The Winds Don't Read"

In retrospect, it doesn't seem that we went too far wrong in the planning and execution of our passage, but there is nearly always something to be learned from such an experience, and our case was no exception. The following is a short list of mistakes, items neglected, or things I would do differently next time.

(1) I now feel that I overdid it in telling Sally about the misadventures that have befallen small-boat offshore sailors. My purpose was to inform her and let her know what to prepare for ahead of time. I wanted her thoughts on how we should ready ourselves for any eventuality, but the horror stories gave her too many misgivings. Also, I should have been more selective in the books I suggested she read. There are more than a few cruise stories that strike a happy medium between being too casual and overplaying the dangers.

(2) The rudder stock stuffing box should have been inspected and repacked before the cruise. I blame myself for neglecting this, because I remembered that Sandro Vitelli had a leak from

this source when he ran into heavy weather while delivering *Kelpie* to Cape May in the fall of 1973. After that, the packing gland was tightened, and I thought this would take care of it. But during our big gale when the stern was slamming, water poured in. I was able to tighten the gland somewhat eventually and slow the water inflow, but repacking at sea was all but impossible, because this would have required removal of the steering quadrant and cables. The job was difficult enough in the boatyard after *Kelpie* returned home.

(3) I would advise very careful inspection of the engine exhaust pipe at the point where it joins the manifold. During our passage a small crack appeared at the joint. Apparently, this is not an uncommon trouble with flexible-mounted engines that are subject to a lot of vibration, because the engine moves but the exhaust tries to hold still. We had duct tape that could have been wrapped around a crack in the pipe but not around the joint at the exhaust manifold. Our problem was not serious, but it caused smoke and a great accumulation of soot in the engine compartment that was very difficult to clean up when *Kelpie* arrived home.

(4) We had ample hand holds, safety belts, lee cloths, safety pins for drawers and bunks, rounded corners on semi-bulkheads and tables, etc., to avoid injury from falls. However, I neglected padding on the porthole dogs. During one of the gales, Rip was thrown against one of the opening ports, and he just missed hitting his head against the thumb screw of the dog. Had he hit it, he would have been seriously injured. A rubber cane tip or similar padding would have afforded protection.

(5) We should have had new gaskets in the opening ports. I squirted a moderately high pressure hose against the closed ports to test them for leaks before we left, but that was not enough. In heavy weather while lying ahull, seas can break aboard with unbelievable force, and in those conditions our opening ports leaked. The glass in one of the ports cracked during a gale, but I'm sure the cause was my overtightening the dogs in an attempt to stop the leaking.

(6) Although I knew we should have them, I did not insist on

strum boxes (strainers) at the ends of the intake hoses on the pumps. This was a mistake, because we had occasional troubles with the pumps clogging despite a thorough cleaning of the bilge. Ed Karkow had trouble with one of the diaphragm pumps (a Whale) that was merely caused by a blister of paint that prevented a vacuum from being formed inside the diaphragm. Although a strum box would not have helped in that particular case, the difficulty illustrates the sensitivity to debris being sucked in.and breaking the vacuum.

(7) A seemingly minor omission from our stores that proved to be major was paper plates. Sally did not like the idea of needlessly polluting the ocean, and she did not really think we would need paper plates. We each had a large flat-bottomed bowl (made by Yachting Tableware Co.) with a rubber ring on the bottom to make it skid-proof, and this was very practical, but washing it after every meal in salt water was a chore. Rip did the lion's share of dishwashing, because Sally and I had other chores, and Sarah developed a skin rash on her fingers that excused her from putting her hands in salt water. At any rate, biodegradable paper plates and cups would have been a big help.

(8) Our experiment of freezing water in polyethylene bags, first using the water for ice and then for emergency drinking, was not a great success. Two out of the three bags, sold as folding water jugs by L. L. Bean, leaked after the ice had thawed. Perhaps the bags were too roughly treated. Actually, we did not lose the water, because it ran into an ice water sump; but anyone using this plan should be sure the water will not be lost through drainage into the bilge in the event the containers leak.

(9) I'd suggest setting a departure date about a month ahead of the time one actually plans to leave on a voyage, in order that all jobs can be completed well in advance and there is ample opportunity to test new equipment. Time and again offshore cruises are begun before the boat is completely ready. In our case the last job to be done, the completion of the emergency rudder stock, was finished on the day we left, and this meant we didn't have time to swing ship properly after the steel rudder stock was stowed. I think this caused some compass

deviation that affected our dead reckoning. Our storm slides were fortunately made well in advance, because they warped, and we were able to correct this by having splines added on each side before we left (see Chapter 3).

(10) Next time, I'll probably leave on our folding propeller rather than change it for one that is larger and solid. Our 14-inch-diameter folding Michigan prop with 10-inch pitch causes much less drag and seems to work just as efficiently as the 16-inch solid prop with 10-inch pitch that we carried on the cruise. I was afraid that the folding prop would become clogged with barnacles on a long passage and fail to open, but now I don't think that would be a problem as long as the engine was run for a short while every few days. The unpainted prop and shaft, coated with a product called Sea-Film, were remarkably free of barnacles when *Kelpie* returned home. Incidentally, our bottom paint, Woolsey Neptune 710, did an excellent job of keeping the bottom clean.

(11) I have no complaints about our sails except that the jiffy reef cringles, installed not long before we left, should have been more strongly reinforced with heavier patches and tapes that bisected the clew. Also, we should have had a proper phantom jib type of spinnaker net, because Ed Karkow got a bad head-stay wrap while carrying the 'chute in the tradewinds. As said earlier, I have never felt the modern parachute spinnaker is a seagoing sail for cruising, but if it is carried at sea when short-handed, there should be a proper net.

Because of the gales we experienced, some people have asked if we didn't make a mistake in our choice of route. I really don't think so, but of course we would have considered going by way of Bermuda if time had been no object. *Kelpie* is a sailboat with a small engine that is very limited in power and range, and the route farther south would have increased our chances of being becalmed. Then too, it would have been a great temptation to linger in Bermuda. I felt we had to be sufficiently far north to get well into the prevailing westerly winds but not so far as to increase our chances of bad weather. The pilot chart for June says, "South of the 40th parallel, gales are seldom encountered. " So we tried to keep just south of the 40th, although we went slightly north of it on one occasion.

Route planning in the north Atlantic can rarely be done with any certainly. I heard of a 24-foot sloop that sailed from Bermuda to the Azores in 16 days, but I also know of a 40-foot sloop and a 50-foot ketch each of which took 22 days to make the same passage. One can never tell for sure. It must be remembered that the pilot charts merely give percentages, and they are not intended for actual prognostication. As H.G. Hasler, the noted singlehander, once observed, "The winds don't read the pilot charts." Another year, taking the same route, we might not encounter any gales at all. In planning any passage, one can do no better than to play the odds and be prepared for anything. I really wanted to leave during the middle of June rather than early in the month in order to increase our chances of avoiding late-spring gales, but had we done so, we might have encountered Amy, the first hurricane of the season. We were approaching the Azores when Amy was near Bermuda.

The general conclusion reached by all of us concerning the merits of the cruise was that it was a valuable and rewarding experience. Not all of it was fun, but most of it was, and the unpleasant moments were unimportant when compared with the net worth. As a matter of fact, after such an experience, one tends to remember the best and forget the worst. When Sally was in her lowest state of mind during the trip, she said, "If I ever get off this boat, I'll never get on another." But after we had returned home, she began hoping that we would have to bring *Kelpie* back from Bermuda. Now she talks so ecstatically about the cruise that I think she has entirely forgotten the bad times.

Part of the rewards of our cruise came from the personal sense of accomplishment and the fulfillment of an urge to do something just a bit different. Although our particular lives were probably more varied than most people's, there is an insipid monotony in the typical day-by-day routine of modern man. Most of the time, our civilization is all but suffocating in the way it protects us from nature, and many of us desire, perhaps

The last sunset as Kelpie approaches Fayal with her ensign flying.

subconsciously, some *cautious* exposure to the elements and a feeling of self-sufficiency. Not that *Kelpie*'s crew were blood-and-thunder adventurers—far from it—but we were not quite ready to become hothouse plants. We needed something to stir the tired blood, awaken the spirit, and start the flow of adrenaline. Again, I don't want to imply any greatness in what we did. It was a very minor doing, but one that afforded us great satisfaction.

As I said before, we learned not only about practical matters of seamanship and navigation, but also about each other and ourselves. There were subtle changes in our philosophy and self-confidence, especially after weathering the heaviest gale. Rip spoke of having a new outlook on life, of coming to realize its fragility and how we should make the most of it, never wasting a precious moment. Sarah said, "I discovered I could keep my wits about me. I think if something out of the ordinary happens again, I'll be able to cope." Sally showed a great deal of courage, because she had definite fears of storms and whales, yet she always had control of herself. She made herself a promise that if we survived, she would be kind to everyone, including her mother-in-law. So far, I think she has kept her word (her treatment of your author possibly excepting).

Sally and I both learned about the pleasure and value of a husband and wife working so closely together on a project. For more than a year before the trip, we planned, schemed, talked about, and collaborated on the preparations. We swapped books, read catalogs, bought gear, exchanged ideas, and studied navigation together. In fact, the planning and execution of the cruise made us closer than we have ever been. However, there is one

possible danger for which a married team working so closely for such a period of time should be alert, and that is the psychological letdown after the project has been concluded.

It is my sincere hope that this book has been of some value and given at least a little encouragement to those who are toying with the idea of a first-time ocean cruise. The great Joshua Slocum once wrote, "To young men contemplating a voyage I would say go." Nothing much can be added to that except to say that with proper planning and the right boat, older men and women as well can go.

INDEX

Italicized page numbers indicate illustrations.